"Say and Do" Grammar Game Boards Fun Sheets

A Companion Book to the "Say and Do®" Grammar Game Boards

Written by Joanne DeNinno and Kim Gill
Edited by Molly DeShong, Keri Spielvogle, and Thomas Webber

Copyright ©2002, SUPER DUPER® PUBLICATIONS, a division of Super Duper®, Inc. All rights reserved. Permission is granted for the user to reproduce the material contained herein in limited form for classroom use only. Reproduction of this material for an entire school or school system is strictly prohibited. No part of this material may be reproduced (except as noted above), stored in a retrieval system, or transmitted in any form or by any means (mechanically, electronically, recording, web, etc.) without the prior written consent and approval of Super Duper® Publications.

www.superduperinc.com
1-800-277-8737

ISBN 978-1-58650-222-5

Dedication

This book is dedicated to the young men in our lives:
Timmy, Chris, Danny, and Matt

We appreciate your interest and enthusiasm in all our publishing endeavors. Your spirit, laughter, and patience mean more to us than you'll ever know.

Thanks, guys! We love you!!

Introduction

"Say and Do"® Grammar Game Board Fun Sheets is a resource book designed to accompany Super Duper's **"Say and Do"® Grammar Game Boards**. The fun sheets target a variety of grammatical structures:

Regular plurals	Regular past tense
Irregular plurals	Irregular past tense
Noun derivation	Noun verb agreement with has/have
Adjective derivation	Possessive nouns
Present tense third person	Passive tense
Noun/verb agreement with is/are	Comparatives and superlatives

Grammar Game Board Fun Sheets supplement the Grammar Game Boards you have selected for your language session. **Grammar Game Board Fun Sheets** are also valuable as homework assignments to reinforce target objectives. The materials are ready to use with minimal preparation for both individual and group therapy or homework. The book includes a variety of games, coloring, listening activities, cut and paste pages, sorting tasks, crosswords, word searches, and other exciting activities.

Each chapter has a total of 17 activities for each game board. Activities 1-10 include words taken directly from the selected game board. Activities 11-17 target the same grammatical structure using additional words. This provides an opportunity for a lot of practice for your students.

Your students will enjoy reaching their grammar goals and objectives with **"Say and Do"® Grammar Game Boards** and **Grammar Game Board Fun Sheets**. Teachers, therapists, students, and parents will have fun working and learning together.

Table of Contents

Groovy Groceries (Game Board 1) 1-18

Regular Plurals

Supermarket Sort 2	Singular-Plural Grocery Sort 11
Draw a Plural 3	Add the Ending-Word Search 12
Groovy Groceries Fill-In 4	Hide the Coupon 13
Groovy Groceries Spinner 5	Scales Sort 14
Supermarket Tic-Tac-Toe 6	Drop a Penny 15
Singular-Plural Memory Game 7	Say and Color Shopping List 16
Supermarket Scene 8	Let's Eat! 17
Supermarket Maze 9	Let's Get Ready for Our Vacation 18
Singular-Plural Groceries Sort 10	

Irregular Island (Game Board 2) 19-36

Irregular Plurals

Singular-Plural Memory Game 20	Fishing for Singular and Plural 29
Shell Collecting Time 21	Let's Listen for Plurals 30
Seagulls and Fish Match 22	Message in a Bottle 31
Make a Scene 23	Irregular Plurals Tic-Tac-Toe 32
Island Maze 24	Singular and Plural Matching 33
Singular-Plural Palm Tree 25	Irregular Island Rescue 34
Shell Necklace 26	Irregular Plurals Cut and Paste Shells 35
Irregular Island Treasure 27	Irregular Plural Sentence 36
Island Word Search 28	

Job Fair (Game Board 3) 37-54

Noun Derivation

When I Grow Up 38	Check Your List! 47
Ride the Bus to the Job Fair 39	Follow Job Fair Directions 48
Job Fair Desks 40	It's Time to Deliver the Mail 49
Job Fair Memory 41	Job Fair Puzzle Fun 50
Sentence Completion 42	Job Fair Puzzle Fun 51
Job Fair Tic-Tac-Toe 43	Photographer Fun 52
To Whom Does This Item Belong? 44	Juggling Fun 53
It's Time to Get Ready for Work 45	Who Said That? 54
Job Search 46	

Sunny Day Fun (Game Board 4) 55-72

Adjective Derivation

A Day at the Beach 56	Fill in the Adjective 65
Sunny Day Scene 57	Sunny Day Match 66
Sunny Day Tic-Tac-Toe 58	Sunny Day Coloring 67
Sunny Day Cut and Paste 59	Sunny Day Starfish 68
Sunny Day Spinner 60	Can You Find It? 69
Sunny Day Memory 61	Sunny Day Word Search 70
Let's Go To the Beach Crossword 62	Let's Eat 71
Let's Fly A Kite 63	Sunny Day Cube 72
Name One More 64	

Table of Contents

Fun on the Farm (Game Board 5) 73-90

Third Person Present Tense

Third Person Present Tense Memory Game................74	Add a Patch..83
Corn in the Bushel 75	Help Farmer Freida Stack-Em-Up.......................84
Third Person Verb Tic-Tac-Toe..76	Roll-A-Verb..85
Third Person Present Tense Spinner Activity.............77	Present Tense Farm Scene....................................86
Third Person Present Tense Puzzle 78	Plow the Field Race 87
Third Person Present Tense Puzzle 79	Happy Piggy-Sad Piggy 88
Color a Can 80	What's Missing? 89
Color the Correct Chicken 81	Fun on the Farm..90
Third Person Present Tense Crossword......................82	

Is and Are Playground (Game Board 6)....................................... 91-108

Is/Are

Is/Are Tic-Tac-Toe..92	Fill in Is/Are...101
Is/Are Memory Game 93	Is/Are Scene...102
Is or Are Puzzle 94	Sliding with Is/Are 103
Puzzle Fun...95	Shoot for the Hoop 104
Is/Are Match Up 96	Yummy Popsicle Fun 105
Is/Are Fun on the Monkey Bars 97	Drop-a-Penny 106
Is/Are Spinner Activity 98	Silly Scene..107
Listening for Is or Are 99	Is/Are Cut and Paste..108
Is/Are Ice Cream Cones..100	

Circus Tense (Game Board 7).. 109-126

Regular Past Tense Verbs

Regular Past Tense Tic-Tac-Toe 110	Memory 119
Popcorn Time 111	Circus Charades..120
Sentence Completion 112	Color the Juggler's Plates 121
Let's Clown Around 113	Listening for Past Tense 122
Peanuts for Penelope 114	Make a Clown..123
Spinner Game 115	Walk the Tightrope Race..................................124
Come to the Big Top Circus 116	Circus Flags Cut and Paste 125
Circus Scene 117	Circus Crossword..126
Follow the Circus Path 118	

Construction Junction (Game Board 8)................................... 127-144

Irregular Past Tense

Hard Hat Fun 128	Past or Present Spinner Activity 137
Irregular Past Tense Tic-Tac-Toe.............................129	Construction Word Search 138
Irregular Past Tense Spinner Activity.....................130	Circle a Word 139
Memory for Irregular Past Tense.............................131	Irregular Past Tense Puzzle.....................................140
Find the Hammer 132	Puzzle Fun...141
Make Your Own Bulldozer 133	Irregular Past Tense Maze 142
Cut and Paste Sentence Completion 134	Build-a-House 143
Help Trudy Build a Wall 135	Irregular Verb Match 144
Color the End of the Wrench 136	

Table of Contents

Sports Talk (Game Board 9) 145-162

Has/Have

Sports Talk Memory Game 146
Sports Man.. 147
Sports Talk Spinner 148
Have/Has Tic-Tac-Toe 149
Have/Has Locker... 150
Have/Has Locker Cards 151
Sports Talk Coloring 152
Sports Day 153
Have/Has Olympics... 154

Move the Football Up the Field 155
Sports Talk Gym Bag.. 156
Tennis Anyone?... 157
Sports Talk Listening.. 158
Have/Has Bats 159
Search... 160
Fisherman's Maze... 161
Double Spinner Fun 162

Bring Your Pet to School (Game Board 10)............................. 163-180

Possessive Nouns

Whose Is It? Animal Match.................................... 164
Tim and Molly Cut and Paste 165
Pet Day Spinner 166
Flip and Find.. 167
Pet Day Adventure.. 168
Circle and Say.. 169
Pet Day Puzzle 170
Pet Day Puzzle 171
Add One More 172

Pet Day Show and Tell... 173
Write the Possessive 174
Pet Day Match.. 175
Pet Day Lost and Found 176
Following Directions on Pet Day 177
Pet Cube 178
Pet Day Game Board 179
Drop-a-Penny.. 180

Under the Stars (Game Board 11)... 181-198

Passive Tense

Form a Passive 182
Passive Fill-Ins 183
More Passive Fill-Ins 184
Match the Picture 185
Paste a Passive 186
Passive Sequencing 187
Passive Tic-Tac-Toe 188
Passive Spinner Activity.. 189
Passive Puzzle Fun 190

Puzzle Fun 191
Camp Scene 192
Passive Memory 193
Color a Star Passive Activity 194
Write a Passive 195
Choose a Picture 196
Ride the Rapids Game 197
Fire and Ice 198

City Scene (Game Board 12) 199-216

Comparatives and Superlatives

"ER" Cut and Paste 200
Comparative/Superlative Game 201
Firehouse Sort.. 202
Comparative/Superlative Tic-Tac-Toe 203
Paste An Ending... 204
Comparative/Superlative Spinner Activity 205
Color Comparative Fun 206
Circle a Word 207
Comparative & Superlative Fill-Ins 208

City Scene-Following Directions............................. 209
Fold a Dog.. 210
Draw a Comparative and Superlative 211
Puzzle Fun 212
Puzzle Fun 213
Color a Superlative 214
Listening for Comparatives & Superlatives 215
Answer Key 216

Parent/Helper Letter

Date: _____

Dear Parent/Homework Helper,

    Your child is currently working on understanding and using correct grammar when speaking and writing. He/She is currently working on _____.

    You can support your child's progress by helping him/her complete the attached activity sheet.

    ☐ Please sign the worksheet below and return it to me by _____.

    ☐ Please complete this sheet at home. It does not need to be returned to me.

    Have fun helping your child understand and use correct grammar!

Thank you,

_____   _____
                   Name   Parent/Helper

Supermarket Sort

Directions: Cut out the food pictures below. Say the plurals in each picture and glue/tape or place the picture on the appropriate shopping cart. Then, use the plural word in a sentence. _____

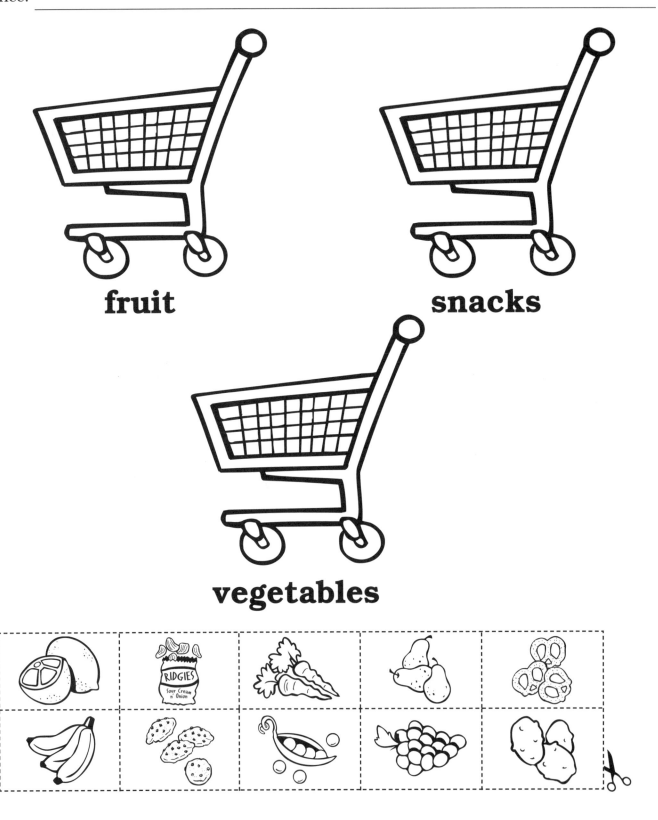

fruit

snacks

vegetables

_____ _____
Homework Partner   Date

Game Board 1
Regular Plurals

Draw a Plural

Directions: Look at the singular picture. Say the plural (apple/apples) of each picture and draw it in the box on the right. Then, use the plural word in a sentence. _____
_____

Homework Partner   Date

Game Board 1
Regular Plurals

Groovy Groceries Fill-In

Directions: Complete each phrase using a word from the Word Bank. Say each phrase in a sentence. If you want, your answers can be silly. _____

1. a **bunch** of _____

2. a **bushel** of _____

3. a **sack** of _____

4. a **carton** of _____

5. a **six-pack** of _____

6. a **slice** from two _____

7. a **box** of _____

8. a **roll** of _____

9. a **bag** of _____

Word Bank

paper towels	cookies	eggs
sodas	potato chips	bananas
pizzas	apples	potatoes

_____ _____
Homework Partner   Date

Game Board 1
Regular Plurals

4   #BK-298 Grammar Game Board Fun Sheets • ©2002 Super Duper® Publications • 1-800-277-8737 • Online! www.superduperinc.com

Groovy Groceries Spinner

Directions: If you prefer, glue this page to construction paper for added durability. Cut out the arrow/dial. Use a brad to connect the dial to the circle. Spin the spinner. Say a sentence using the plural of the picture (bun/buns) indicated on the spinner.

Homework Partner　　　　　　　　　　　Date

Game Board 1
Regular Plurals

Supermarket Tic-Tac-Toe

Directions: Cut out the Tic-Tac-Toe tokens below. One player gets "**shopping carts**" and the other gets "**cash registers**." Take turns covering a picture. Player one picks out a square, uses the plural form of the picture in a sentence, and puts a token on the picture. Player two follows in turn. Three in a row wins! _____

_____ _____
Homework Partner   Date

Game Board 1

Regular Plurals

Singular-Plural Memory Game

Directions: If you prefer, glue this page onto construction paper for added durability. Cut out all of the cards and place them face down on the table. Take turns flipping the cards, trying to match the singular pictures with the plural pictures (pea/peas). Say all the words in sentences. Most matches win!

_____ _____
Homework Partner   Date

Game Board 1

Regular Plurals

Supermarket Scene

Directions: Look at the scene below. How many different plurals can you find? Say the plurals and color each one. (I see some **cans**.)

Word Bank

peas	pots	pears	doughnut
lemons	apples	grapes	pretzels
cups	napkins	mops	potatoes
carrots	potato chips	bananas	tomatoes
paper towels	sodas		lightbulbs
	muffins		
	cookies		

Homework Partner _____ Date _____

Game Board 1
Regular Plurals

8 #BK-298 Grammar Game Board Fun Sheets • ©2002 Super Duper® Publications • 1-800-277-8737 • Online! www.superduperinc.com

Supermarket Maze

Directions: Find your way to the supermarket check out. Say the plural of each item you pass along the way (pear/pears).

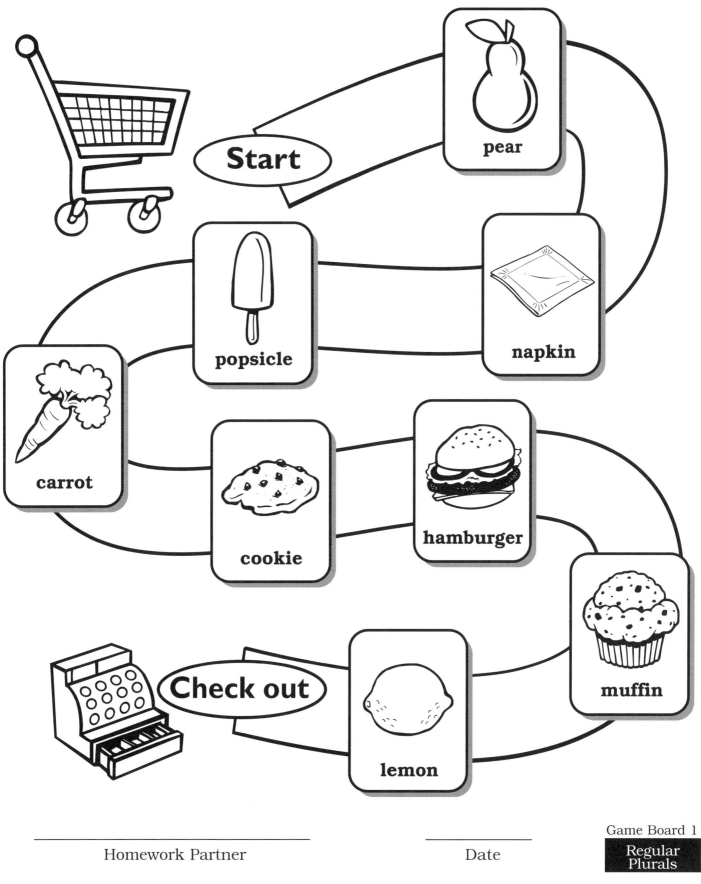

Homework Partner   Date

Game Board 1
Regular Plurals

Singular-Plural Groceries Sort

Directions: Cut the slot on the top of each grocery bag. Then, cut out the picture cards on the following page. Choose a card, say the word and use it in a sentence. Now, place the card in the correct bag. Continue until all the pictures have been sorted.

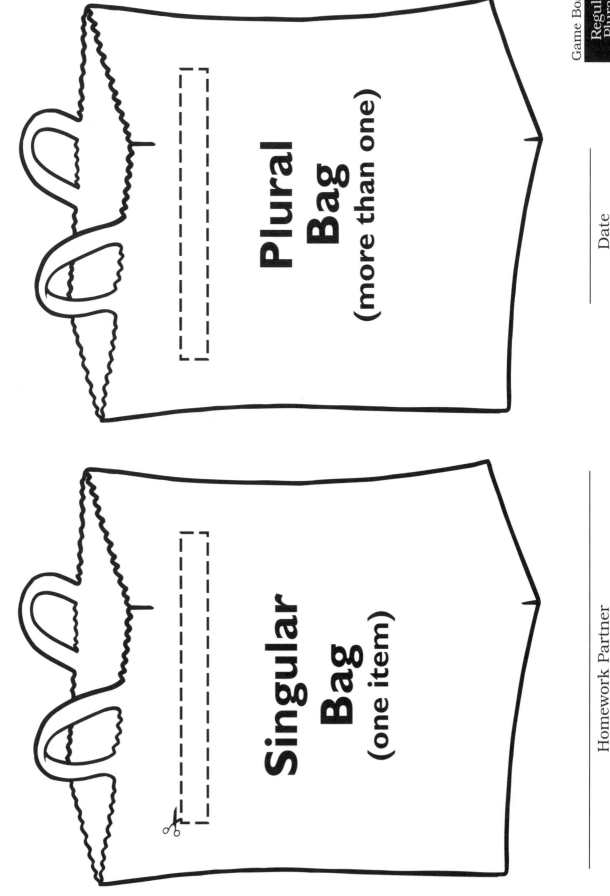

Game Board 1
Regular Plurals

Homework Partner _____ Date _____

Singular-Plural Grocery Sort

Directions: Cut out the pictures below. Then, follow the directions on the previous page.

cookie	hot dog	pots
grapes	batteries	muffin
buns	pizza	cups
pretzel	potato chips	pear

Homework Partner · Date

Add the Ending - Word Search

Directions: Look at the picture clues below. Add the correct plural ending to each word (cupcake_/cupcakes). Find that plural word in the puzzle. Then, say each word in a sentence.

C	S	X	Z	I	B	P	A	C	S	O	K	S
A	D	O	G	B	I	S	C	U	I	T	S	Q
N	C	F	R	E	N	C	H	F	R	I	E	S
D	C	U	P	C	A	K	E	S	P	L	U	X
Y	S	T	P	E	C	S	R	R	I	P	L	S
B	R	T	E	R	T	S	R	A	T	I	I	E
A	B	V	R	E	I	S	I	W	L	N	M	I
R	S	I	R	I	S	T	E	A	K	S	E	Z
S	F	X	M	A	E	W	S	I	R	E	S	A
W	S	T	R	A	W	B	E	R	R	I	E	S

Answer key: p.216

 cherr__ __ __

 dog biscuit__

 candy bar__

 strawberr__ __ __

 cupcake__

 steak__

 lime__

french fr__ __ __

_____ _____
Homework Partner   Date

Hide the Coupon

Directions: If you prefer, glue this page to construction paper for added durability. Cut out the cards and the coupon. Place the cards face down. Close your eyes while your partner hides the coupon under a card. Flip a card and read/say the word. Then, say the plural. Flip cards until you find the coupon. Play again, hiding the coupon for your partner.

Scales Sort

Directions: Cut out the pictures at the bottom of the page. Choose a picture and say the plural of that picture (steak/steaks). Glue/tape or place the picture on the appropriate scale (meats, fruits, or vegetables).

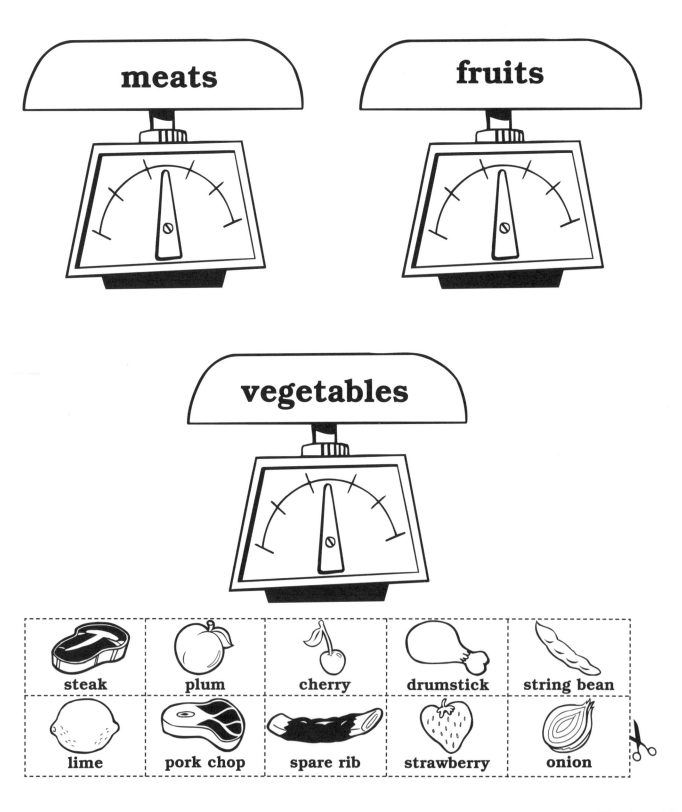

Drop a Penny

Directions: Take a penny and drop it on the page below. Wherever the penny lands, say the word, then say the plural (plum/plums). Then, use the words in sentences.

Say and Color Shopping List

Directions: Can you figure out what items we need from the grocery store? Say the items on the list and color each picture. Then, use each word in a sentence. Use the Word Bank for help.

Word Bank

| jams and jellies | waffles | pies |
| cupcakes | tortilla chips | pancakes |

Things To Buy

1. _____

2. _____

3. _____

4. _____

5. _____

6. _____

_____   _____
Homework Partner   Date

Regular Plurals

Let's Eat!

Directions: Cut out the balloons at the bottom of the page. Look at the word on each balloon and make each word plural by adding an "s" at the end. If you can use that item at your party, glue/tape or place it on a string. Say the words in sentences. Then, color the empty balloons.

rug___ dog biscuit___ candy bar___ onion___

plate___ lollipop___ cupcake___ fork___

Homework Partner   Date

Regular Plurals

Let's Get Ready for Our Vacation

Directions: Read or listen to the story below. Say the plural words that are pictured in the story. For a hint, use the Word Bank.

Word Bank

pancakes	french fries	pies
waffles	tortilla chips	nuts
strawberries	spare ribs	string beans
drumsticks	cupcakes	steaks

It is vacation time! Mom, Pedro and Maria are going to the market to buy some food for their trip. "First, we need breakfast food," said Pedro. "How about some or ?" said Mom. "I like ," said Pedro. "Maria, you can choose lunch," said Mom. "Can we get some  and fresh for dessert?" asked Maria. "Sure!" said Mom, "Dad likes to barbeque for dinner," she added. "Let's get some and ." Maria exclaimed, "Don't forget the veggies! How about  ?" "Yuck!" whined Pedro. "No complaining, Pedro! You can pick some snacks," replied Mom. "Hooray! I pick , , and..." "Okay, that's enough," said Mom. "Look at these ! I'll grab an apple and a blueberry for dessert," said Maria. "I think we're all set," said Mom, "Let's head for the check out, then off we go on our vacation!"

_____   _____
Homework Partner   Date

Singular-Plural Memory Game

Directions: If you prefer, glue this page onto construction paper for added durability. Cut out all of the cards and place them face down on the table. Player one turns over a card and uses the word in a sentence. The player then turns over a second card trying to find its singular or plural match. Use that word in a sentence. Play continues in turn. Most matches win.

Homework Partner   Date

Game Board 2
Irregular Plurals

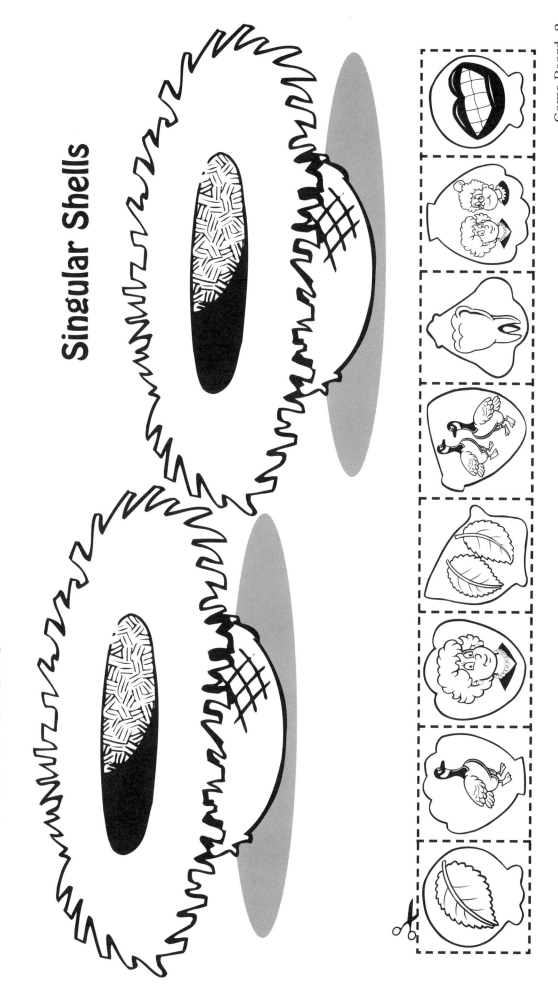

Shell Collecting Time

Directions: Cut out the singular and plural shell pictures at the bottom of the page. Glue/tape or place each shell in the appropriate straw hat. Then, say each word in a sentence.

Singular Shells

Plural Shells

Homework Partner _____ Date _____

Game Board 2
Irregular Plurals

Seagulls and Fish Match

Directions: Help the seagulls find the fish. First, read the singular word on a seagull. Then, try to find the matching irregular plural word on a fish (die/dice). Draw a line from the "singular seagull" to the "plural fish." Say each word in a sentence. Continue until all seagulls have found their fish.

Game Board 2
Irregular Plurals

Homework Partner _____ Date _____

Island Maze

Directions: Help the islanders find their way home! Change each singular word to the plural form as you travel along (mouse/mice). Then, use each plural word in a sentence.

Homework Partner   Date

Game Board 2
Irregular Plurals

Singular-Plural Palm Tree

Directions: Cut out the coconuts at the bottom of the page. Read the singular word on each coconut and change it to the plural form (tooth/teeth). Then, say each word in a sentence and tape/glue or place on the palm tree.

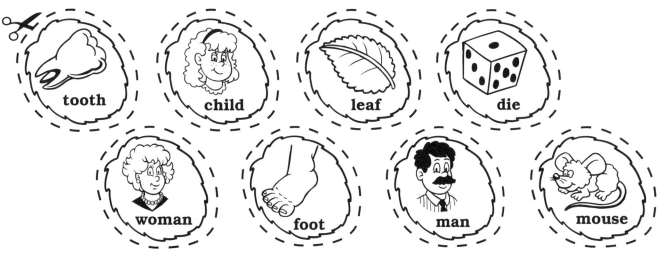

tooth · child · leaf · die
woman · foot · man · mouse

Homework Partner   Date

Game Board 2
Irregular Plurals

Shell Necklace

Directions: Color and cut out the shells at the bottom of the page along the solid line. Fold each shell on the dotted lines. Take a shell and make up sentences using each word on the shell. (My tooth hurts./I will brush my teeth.) Then, glue each shell over a long piece of yarn. Tie the yarn ends together and wear your island necklace.

Homework Partner _____ Date _____

Game Board 2 — Irregular Plurals

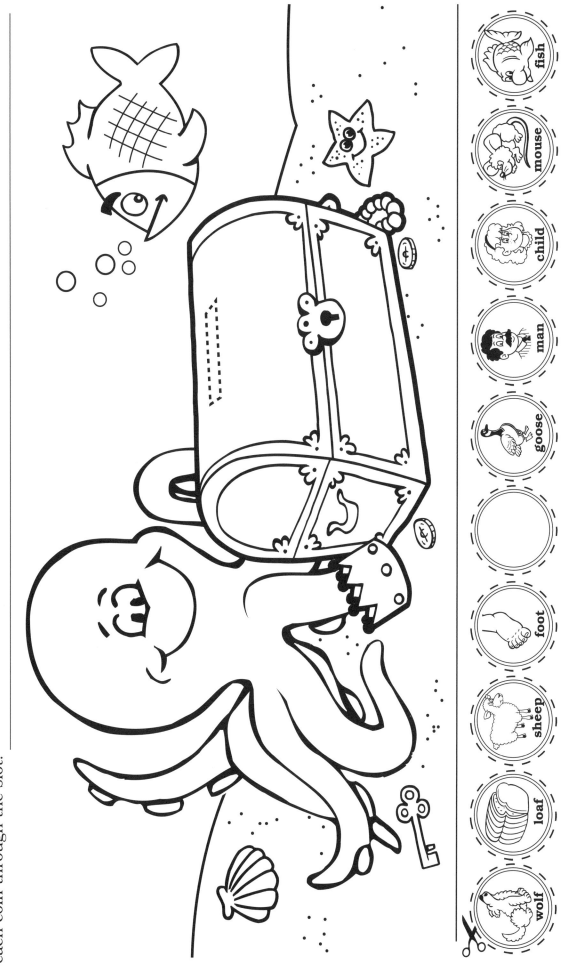

Island Word Search

Directions: Read each singular word. Fill in the spaces next to each word to form the plural (mouse/mice). Some of the letters are already filled in for you! Find the plural words in the puzzle. Then, say each plural word in a sentence.

C	O	M	F	M	T	E	R	M	U	E
Y	S	H	E	E	P	G	W	W	N	B
W	O	M	E	N	Q	G	A	D	P	L
O	S	I	T	E	C	S	T	E	I	P
L	R	C	H	I	L	D	R	E	N	I
V	E	E	T	E	I	I	E	R	L	N
E	S	I	R	I	W	C	A	Y	F	A
S	F	X	M	A	T	E	E	T	H	E

Answer key: p.216

mouse	m _ _ _	tooth	t _ _ t h
man	m _ _	deer	d _ _ _
foot	f _ _ t	sheep	s h _ _ p
wolf	w o l _ _ _	child	c h i l d r _ _
woman	w o _ _ n	die	d i _ _

Homework Partner   Date

Game Board 2
Irregular Plurals

Let's Listen for Plurals

Directions: Read or listen to each sentence. If the sentence is correct, color the smiling starfish. If the sentence is incorrect, color the frowning starfish. Then, say the sentence correctly.

1. The toys are on the two middle <u>shelves</u>.

2. Many <u>elfs</u> worked in the toy shop.

3. Three baby <u>calves</u> drank milk.

4. Place all the <u>knives</u> on the table.

5. Two <u>oxes</u> can pull a heavy load.

6. A horse has four <u>hoofs</u>.

7. "Children, wear your <u>scarves</u>," said Mom.

8. Two <u>thieves</u> robbed a bank.

9. Three <u>firemans</u> put out the fire.

10. Some <u>policewomen</u> wear badges.

_____ _____
Homework Partner   Date

Message in a Bottle

Directions: Cut out the words at the bottom of the page. Read each word and decide if it's singular or plural. Then glue/tape or place a plural word in each bottle and throw the singular words away. Say the plural words in sentences.

| hooves | elf | thieves | calves | policewomen |
| wives | oxen | knives | scarf | firemen |

Homework Partner   Date

Irregular Plurals

Irregular Plurals Tic-Tac-Toe

Directions: Cut out the Tic-Tac-Toe tokens below. One player gets "**X**'s" and the other gets the "**O**'s." Player one picks out a square, says the word, and changes it to the plural form (shelf-shelves). Player one puts a token on the picture. Second player follows in turn. Three in a row wins.

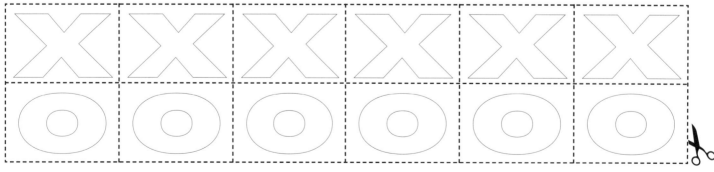

Homework Partner   Date

Irregular Plurals

Singular and Plural Matching

Directions: Draw lines to match each singular picture on the left to its matching plural picture on the right. Say/write the plural word on the line next to the picture on the right. Use each word in a sentence. (I see a moose./I see two moose.)

moose

shelf

fireman

soap

elf

_____   _____
Homework Partner   Date

Irregular Plurals

Irregular Island Rescue

Directions: Cut out the word strip on the right side of the page. Make a slot by cutting on the dotted line near the bottom of the helicopter. Slip the word strip through the slot from the bottom of your paper. Say each word as you pull the rescue ladder down towards the island. Change each word to its plural form (elf/elves) and use it in a sentence.

| elf | shelf | wife | thief | scarf | hoof | knife | calf |

Irregular Plurals

Homework Partner _____ Date _____

Irregular Plurals Cut and Paste Shells

Directions: Color and cut out the pictures at the top of the page. Glue each one in the matching box at the bottom of the page. Say each word in a sentence.

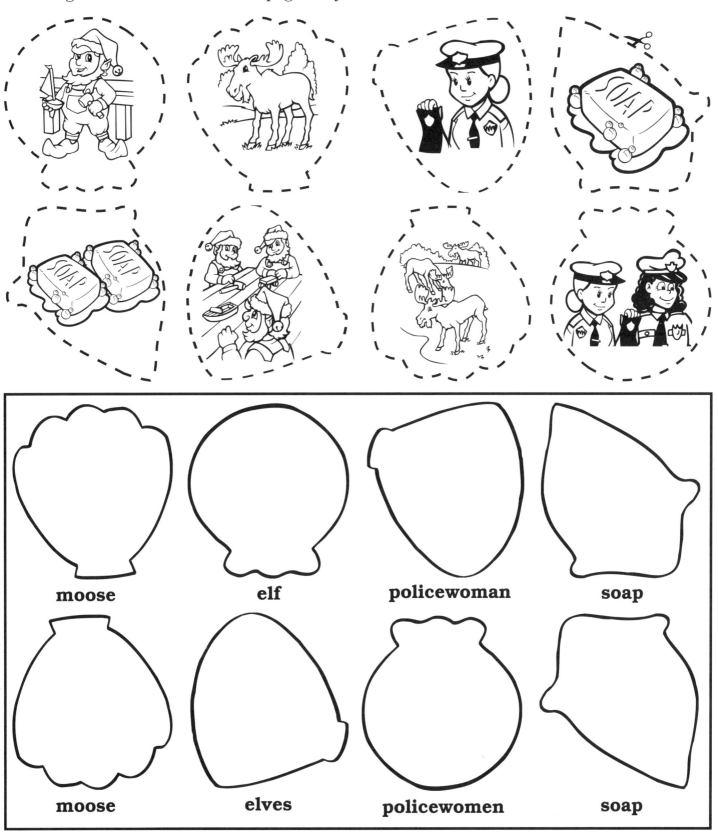

#BK-298 Grammar Game Board Fun Sheets • ©2002 Super Duper® Publications • 1-800-277-8737 • Online! www.superduperinc.com

Irregular Plural Sentence

Directions: Cut out the pictures at the bottom of the page. Read each sheet and glue/tape or place each picture in the appropriate box to correctly complete the sentence. Then read each completed sentence. _____

1. I bought three bars of ☐ .

2. When it is cold, children wear ☐ .

3. The mother cows fed their baby ☐ .

4. Put your books on the two top ☐ .

5. Many ☐ rode in the fire truck.

6. We saw a herd of ☐ in the woods.

7. Two ☐ arrested the robber.

8. Four ☐ pulled the wagon.

calves | policewomen | soap | scarves | oxen | shelves | firemen | moose

_____ _____
Homework Partner   Date

Irregular Plurals

When I Grow Up

Directions: Decide what you might be when you grow up. Choose one of the words below and write it in the first blank. Then, use your own words to fill in the rest of the blanks. Read your story aloud. _____

When I grow up, I might be a _____. I will wear _____. Some items I will use at my job are _____ and _____. The place where I will work is called a _____. At my job, I will do many things. One of these things might be _____ _____. I will like my job because _____ _____. I can't wait to be a _____.

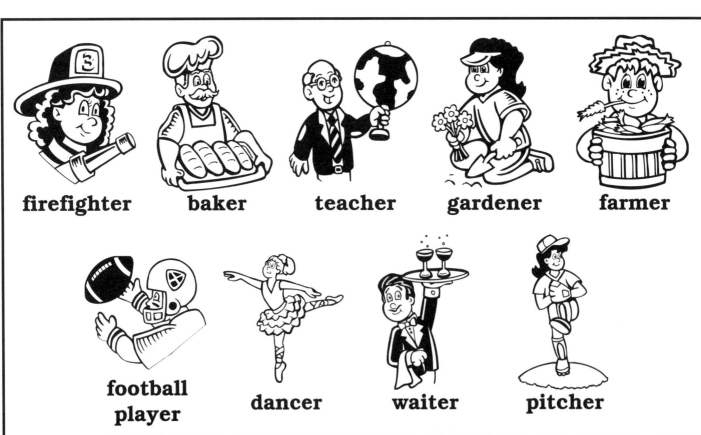

firefighter   baker   teacher   gardener   farmer

football player   dancer   waiter   pitcher

Homework Partner   Date

Game Board 3

Noun Derivation

Ride the Bus to the Job Fair

Directions: Cut out the pictures at the bottom of the page. Name each picture and glue/tape or place it in a window on the bus. If you need a hint, use the words around the bus.

welder
sailor
actor
painter
singer
bus driver
surfer
football player

Homework Partner _____ Date _____

Game Board 3
Noun Derivation

#BK-298 Grammar Game Board Fun Sheets • ©2002 Super Duper® Publications • 1-800-277-8737 • Online! www.superduperinc.com   39

Job Fair Desks

Directions: Cut out the worker cards along the dotted lines. Look at the pictures of the workers. Glue the correct worker card on his/her desk. Use each one in a sentence. (The pitcher threw the ball.)

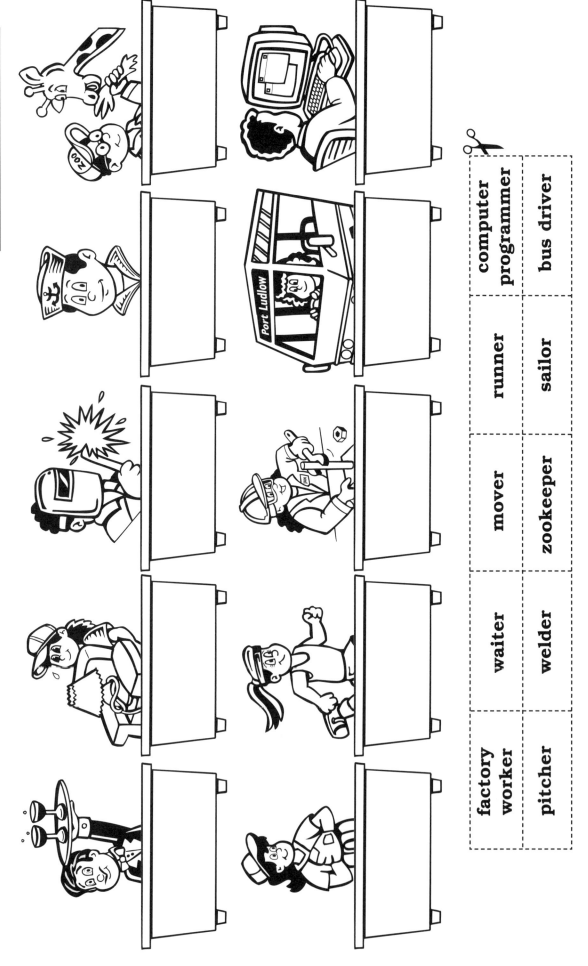

factory worker	waiter	mover	runner	computer programmer
pitcher	welder	zookeeper	sailor	bus driver

Homework Partner _____ Date _____

Game Board 3
Noun Derivation

Job Fair Memory

Directions: If you prefer, glue this page onto construction paper for added durability. Cut out all of the cards and place them face down on the table. Player turns over two cards, reads/says the cards aloud, and tries to match the person with the object he/she uses at his/her job. The player keeps any matches. Play continues in turn. Most matches win.

Sentence Completion

Directions: Read each sentence. Fill in each blank with a noun from the Word Bank. Use the pictures for hints. You can also use these cards to play a sentence/picture memory game.

Word Bank

teacher	mover	waiter	baker	firefighter
ice skater	builder	farmer	zookeeper	runner

The _____ loaded the moving van.	The _____ milked the cows.	The _____ took the food order.	The _____ hammered the nail.	The _____ measured the flour.
The _____ laced her skates.	The _____ fed the animals.	The _____ drove the fire truck.	The _____ ran around the track.	The _____ taught the students.

Homework Partner _____   Date _____

Game Board 3

Job Fair Tic-Tac-Toe

Directions: Cut out the Tic-Tac-Toe markers below. One player gets "**fire hats**" and the other gets "**baker hats**." Player one covers a picture, naming the person, and something he/she uses at work. Player two follows in turn. Three in a row wins! _____

Homework Partner _____ Date _____

Game Board 3

Noun Derivation

#BK-298 Grammar Game Board Fun Sheets • ©2002 Super Duper® Publications • 1-800-277-8737 • Online! www.superduperinc.com

To Whom Does This Item Belong?

Directions: Below you will see pictures of items that belong to a particular worker. Find the name of the worker in the Word Bank and write it on the line below each item. Then, make up a sentence about each one. (The baker made a cake.)

Word Bank

teacher	dancer	baker	computer programmer
ice skater	painter	football player	firefighter
singer	builder	surfer	farmer

Game Board 3

Noun Derivation

It's Time to Get Ready for Work

Directions: Cut out the pictures at the bottom of the page. Glue/tape or place each one on the correct person. Say sentences using "dancer" and "singer." (The dancer wears a crown.)

Homework Partner   Date

Game Board 3
Noun Derivation

Job Search

Directions: Cut out the pictures at the bottom of the page. Read each job description and glue/tape or place each picture in the correct box. Name each job/worker. (Someone who plants crops-farmer.) _____

CLASSIFIED

WANTED: Someone who can lift furniture.

WANTED: Someone who plants crops.

WANTED: Someone who takes care of animals.

WANTED: Someone who stands on a mound.

WANTED: Someone who rides the waves.

WANTED: Someone who bakes bread and cookies.

WANTED: Someone who tends the flowers.

Homework Partner _____ Date _____

Game Board 3
Noun Derivation

Check Your List!

Directions: Read the three words on each list. Choose the name of the worker from the Word Bank that would go with that list. Then, write it on the line at the top and use it in a sentence. Continue until you fill in all of the lists.

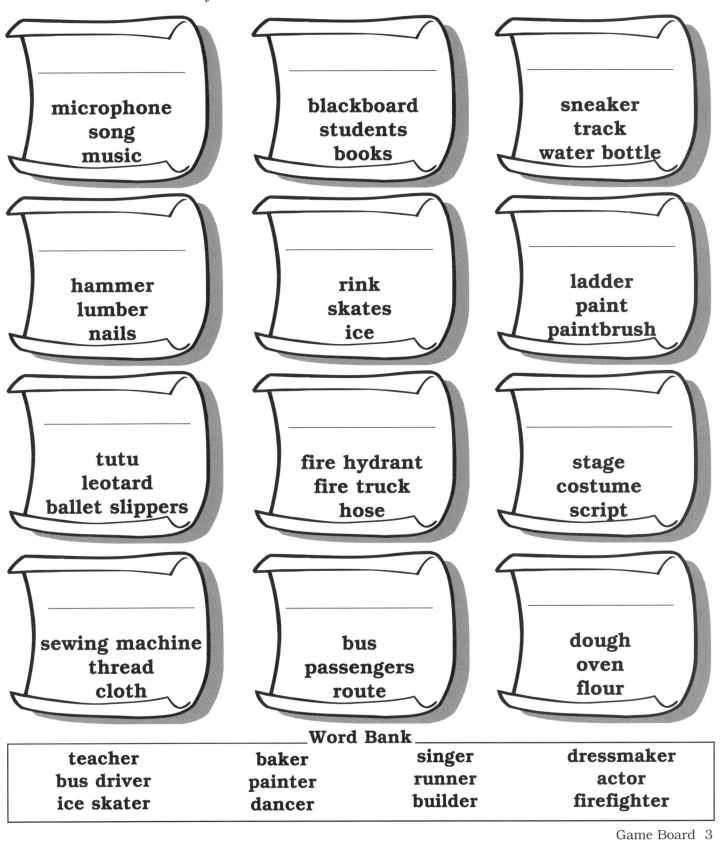

microphone	blackboard	sneaker
song	students	track
music	books	water bottle

hammer	rink	ladder
lumber	skates	paint
nails	ice	paintbrush

tutu	fire hydrant	stage
leotard	fire truck	costume
ballet slippers	hose	script

sewing machine	bus	dough
thread	passengers	oven
cloth	route	flour

Word Bank

teacher	baker	singer	dressmaker
bus driver	painter	runner	actor
ice skater	dancer	builder	firefighter

Homework Partner   Date

Game Board 3

Noun Derivation

Follow Job Fair Directions

Directions: Look at the pictures below. Circle the people who play a sport. Cross out the people who entertain an audience. Draw a square around the people who help around the house. Then, say a sentence about each one.

Homework Partner   Date

Noun Derivation

It's Time to Deliver the Mail

Directions: Help the mail carrier deliver mail to the other workers. Name the item pictured on each envelope and tell who uses it to do his/her job. (A swimmer uses a pool.) For a hint, use the Word Bank.

Word Bank

swimmer	golfer
juggler	writer
photographer	drummer
window washer	housekeeper
baseball player	soccer player

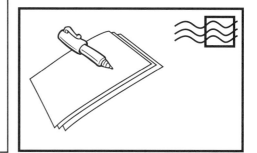

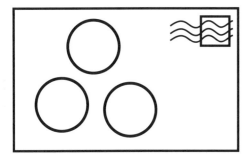
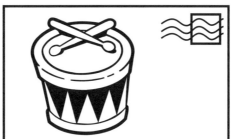
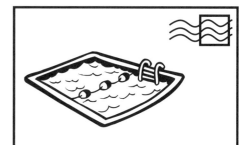

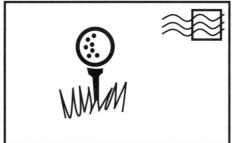

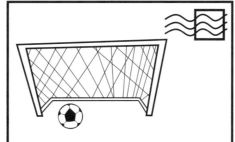
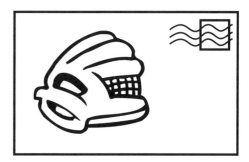

Homework Partner   Date

Noun Derivation

Job Fair Puzzle Fun

Directions: Cut out the puzzle pieces on page 51. Shuffle and place face down. Pick a puzzle piece and find the person who uses that item on this page. Match the two pictures together. For more fun, glue the pictures to this page.

Homework Partner   Date

Noun Derivation

Job Fair Puzzle Fun

Directions: Cut out and shuffle the puzzle pieces below. Follow the directions on page 50.

_____ _____
Homework Partner   Date

Noun Derivation

Photographer Fun

Directions: The photographer is taking pictures of different places. Make up sentences using the worker and the place. (An actor works on a stage.)

Homework Partner   Date

Noun Derivation

Juggling Fun

Directions: Cut out the box with the juggler in it, the block directly above the juggler's head, and the wheel on the dotted lines. Using a brad, attach the wheel under the juggler at the X. Look at the picture that appears in the window (block). Tell who might use this object and make up a sentence. (A drummer uses a drum.) Continue until you've seen all pictures.

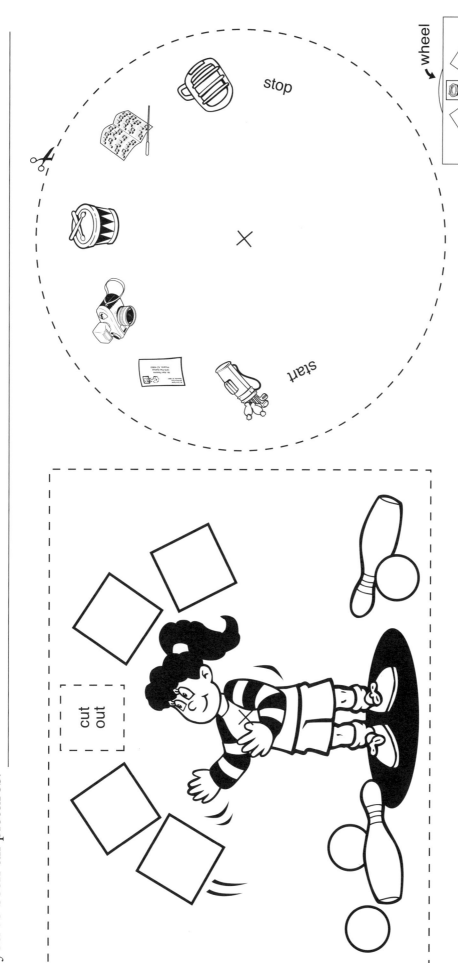

Noun Derivation

Homework Partner _____ Date _____

Who Said That?

Directions: Cut out the speech bubbles at the bottom of the page along the dotted lines. Read each sentence. Glue/tape or place each speech bubble next to the person who would say that sentence. Name each person. (Pitch the ball to me. I am a catcher.) _____

Homework Partner _____ Date _____

Noun Derivation

A Day at the Beach

Directions: Change each word in **BOLD** to an adjective (sun/sunny). Then read your story aloud.

"Let's go, everyone!" called Mom. "It is a perfect beach day. It is very _____ !" Patty and Paul put on their swimsuits and jumped
(**sun**)
into the car with Mom and their dog, Peanuts. Patty and Paul were so happy, they laughed all the way to the beach. "You two are so _____ ,"
(**giggle**)
laughed Mom. Finally, they arrived at the _____ beach and
(**sand**)
spread out their very _____ blanket. Everyone enjoyed a quick
(**lump**)
snack of _____ watermelon and _____ potato chips. After a
(**juice**) (**crunch**)
short rest, _____ Patty, Paul, and _____ Peanuts played in
(**noise**) (**spunk**)
the _____ , _____ waves. Suddenly it got very _____ and
(**salt**) (**foam**) (**cloud**)
_____ . "It is going to be _____ very soon," exclaimed Mom,
(**wind**) (**storm**)
"It is time for us to call it a day!" Everyone ran to the car. Mom, two very _____ kids, and one very _____ dog headed home after
(**sleep**) (**fur**)
all that sunny day fun.

Homework Partner   Date

Game Board 4
Adjective Derivation

Sunny Day Scene

Directions: Find and circle the following adjectives in the scene below: sleepy, stormy, messy, juicy, windy, crunchy, noisy, foamy, grassy, and furry. Then, say each one in a sentence.

Homework Partner _____   Date _____

Game Board 4
Adjective Derivation

Sunny Day Tic-Tac-Toe

Directions: Cut out the Tic-Tac-Toe tokens below. One player gets "**suns**" and the other gets "**kites**." Player one picks out a square, reads the phrase, and changes the underlined word to an adjective (a lot of noise/noisy). Then, he/she puts a token on the picture. Player two follows in turn. Three in a row wins!

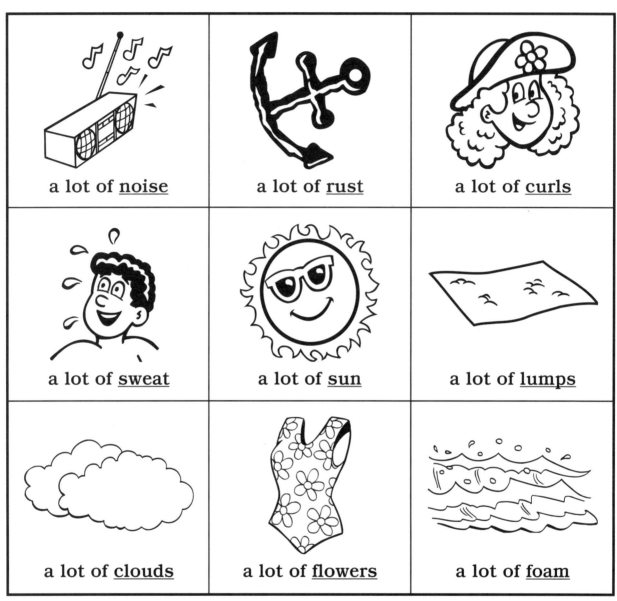

Homework Partner   Date

Game Board 4

Adjective Derivation

Sunny Day Cut and Paste

Directions: Cut out the items at the bottom of the page. Glue each one anywhere in the scene. Change each word to an adjective (sun/sunny). For extra practice, try each adjective in a sentence. (This is a sunny day.)

Game Board 4
Adjective Derivation

grass foam fur rust noise storm crunch sun

Homework Partner _____ Date _____

Sunny Day Spinner

Directions: If you prefer, glue this page onto construction paper for added durability. Cut out the arrow/dial. Use a brad to connect the dial to the circle. Spin the spinner and complete each sentence. (Use the clues around the board if necessary.)

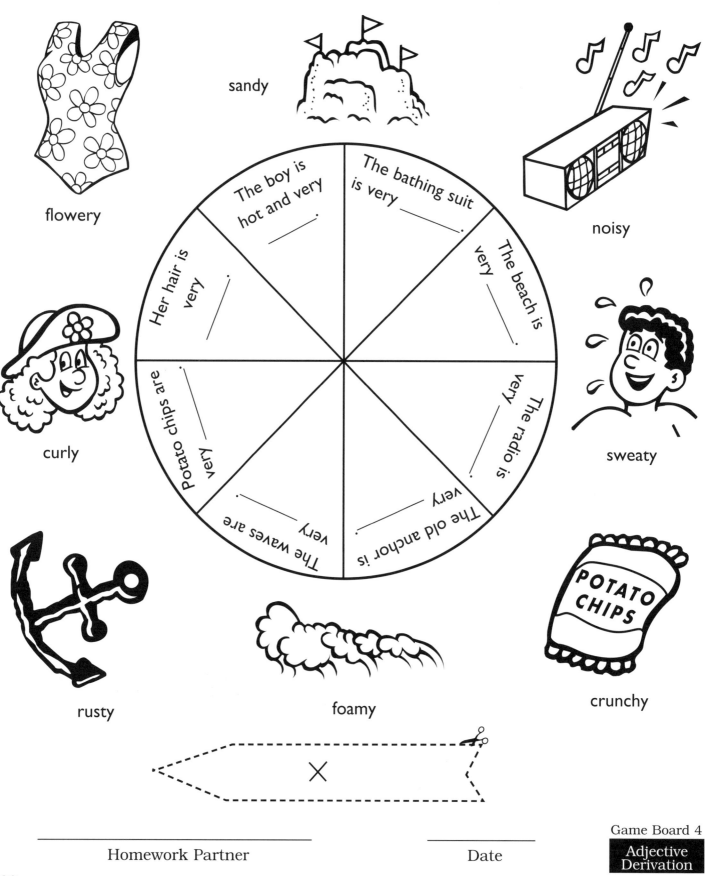

Homework Partner   Date

Game Board 4
Adjective Derivation

Sunny Day Memory

Directions: If you prefer, glue this page onto construction paper for added durability. Cut out all of the cards, divide them into two piles, and place them face down on the table. Take turns flipping one card from each pile trying to match the word to its picture. Keep all matches. Most matches win!

(anchor)	**rusty**	(sandcastle)	**sandy**
(swimsuit)	**flowery**	(kite)	**windy**
(laughing woman)	**giggly**	(blanket)	**lumpy**
(sun over water)	**shiny**	(ice cream on head)	**messy**

Homework Partner   Date

Game Board 4
Adjective Derivation

Let's Go to the Beach Crossword

Directions: Complete each sentence below with the correct adjective. Use the adjectives to complete the puzzle.

Answer Key: ACROSS 1. foamy 3. shady 5. shiny 6. bumpy 8. cloudy DOWN 2. messy 4. salty 5. spunky 7. curly 9. sweaty

ACROSS

1. The waves make a lot of foam. They are very _____.
3. The umbrellas make a lot of shade. It is very _____.
5. The sun makes the water shine. It is very _____.
6. The boat ride had a lot of bumps. It was very _____.
8. There were a lot of clouds. It was very _____.

DOWN

2. The boy made a mess eating ice cream. He is very _____.
4. The ocean has a lot of salt. It is very _____.
5. The dog has a lot of spunk. He is very _____.
7. The girl's hair has a lot of curls. It is very _____.
9. The hot sun is making you sweat. You are very _____.

_____   _____

Homework Partner   Date

Game Board 4
Adjective Derivation

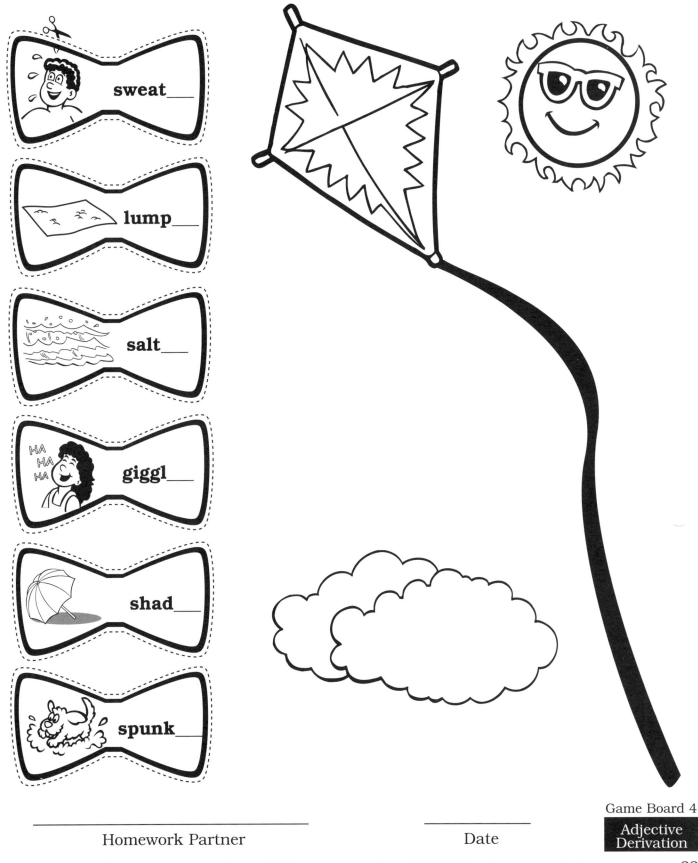

Name One More

Directions: Look at each picture and read each adjective. In the boxes on the right of each picture, draw, write or say another adjective that would describe that picture (juicy – sweet). Say your words in a sentence. _____

 furry		 juicy	
 crunchy		 lumpy	
 flowery		 shiny	
 salty		 noisy	

Homework Partner _____ Date _____

Game Board 4

Adjective Derivation

Fill in the Adjective

Directions: Read or listen to the sentences below. Complete each sentence with the correct adjective using the Word Bank at the bottom of the page. Then, read each sentence aloud.

1. I just finished running a race. I am very _____.

2. There is not a cloud in the sky. It is very _____.

3. The children cannot stop laughing. They are very _____.

4. The boy has not cleaned his room. His room is very _____.

5. The girl stayed up too late. Now she is very _____.

6. Today is a great kite flying day. Today is very _____.

7. The radio and TV are on too loud. It is very _____.

8. If you are too hot you can sit under a tree. Under the tree, it is very_____.

9. There are many holes in the road. The road is very _____.

10. It is raining cats and dogs today. Today, it is very _____.

Word Bank

sunny	sleepy	bumpy	noisy	messy
sweaty	shady	stormy	windy	giggly

Game Board 4

Adjective Derivation

Sunny Day Match

Directions: Draw lines to match the pictures in Column A to the words in Column B. Then, say each word in a sentence. _____

A **B**

pointy

slimy

thirsty

buggy

smelly

rocky

Homework Partner　　　　Date

Adjective Derivation

Sunny Day Coloring

Directions: Color the smelly things green. Color the dirty things red. Color the slimy things blue. Color the lucky things orange. Then, say a sentence about each picture.

Homework Partner   Date

Adjective Derivation

Sunny Day Starfish

Directions: Look at the words on the pointy starfish. Pick a word and say it in a sentence. Color the starfish after you have used all the words in sentences.

Homework Partner Date

Adjective Derivation

Can You Find It?

Directions: Look at the beach scene. Find and circle something: fuzzy, smelly, pointy, slimy, rocky, thirsty, and dirty. Say each adjective in a sentence.

Homework Partner _____   Date _____

Adjective Derivation

Sunny Day Word Search

Directions: Read the sentences at the bottom of the page. Add "y" to each word to make it an adjective (thirst__ – thirsty). Find each adjective in the puzzle. Then, say each adjective in your own sentence. _____

```
L G C R H F B K E V J B V B T
D I O L L O Z L G X B L R N E
N U M O O S Z H U L U O J D T
O T W K Y T M H U N G R Y O P
T E M Z X N H M V M G K F L S
R L H Q T H I R S T Y S N W S
U N J T E L F O S Z E B W V A
M X S N O E U C Y T U L I T L
Q H L K L U C K Y E S R S Y G
W L I X Y C C Y A E J O Q T S
P K M I Q B M O V D P I N L D
P L Y M R I R E V O L C O B I
J W B O I U B M D E X N Q Y R
S R G F L A S H L I G H T D T
H L S Z H R M F Z P O I N T Y
```

Answer key: p.216

1. The boy needs a drink of water. He is very thirst____.
2. There is slime on the seaweed. It is so slim____!
3. There are many rocks on the beach. It is very rock____.
4. You have a winning ticket! You are very luck____.
5. The girl needs a snack. She is very hungr____.
6. There are so many bugs here! It is very bugg____.
7. The starfish have many points. They are very point____.
8. The boy has dirt all over his face. He is very dirt____.

_____ _____
Homework Partner   Date

Adjective Derivation

Let's Eat

Directions: Cut out the hot dogs at the bottom of the page. Then, cut out the space in the boy's face. Say each word in a sentence as you feed the hot dogs to the boy. (The boy was hungry.)

Homework Partner   Date   Speech-Language Pathologist

Adjective Derivation

Sunny Day Cube

Directions: Assemble the cube as follows. Glue onto construction paper for added durability. Cut on the dotted lines. Fold on solid lines and glue as indicated. To play: roll the cube. Look at the picture and word on the top side of the cube. Change the word to an adjective (fuzz/fuzzy) and say a sentence. Keep rolling until you have used each adjective in a sentence.

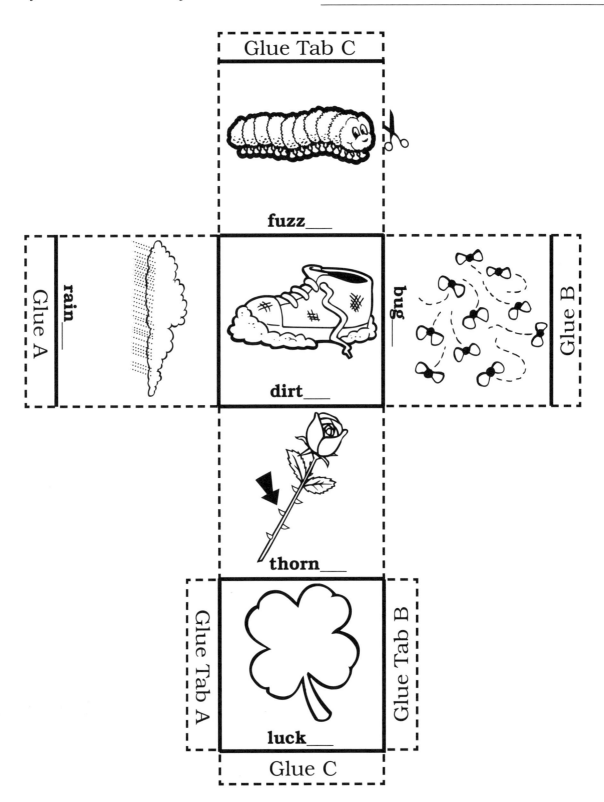

Homework Partner   Date   Speech-Language Pathologist

Adjective Derivation

Third Person Present Tense Memory Game

Directions: If you prefer, glue this page onto construction paper for added durability. Cut out all of the cards and place them face down on the table. Play memory to match the verb pictures. Say a sentence using a third person present tense verb form as you play. (The girl **sleeps** in a bed.) The player keeps any matches. Play continues in turn. Most matches win.

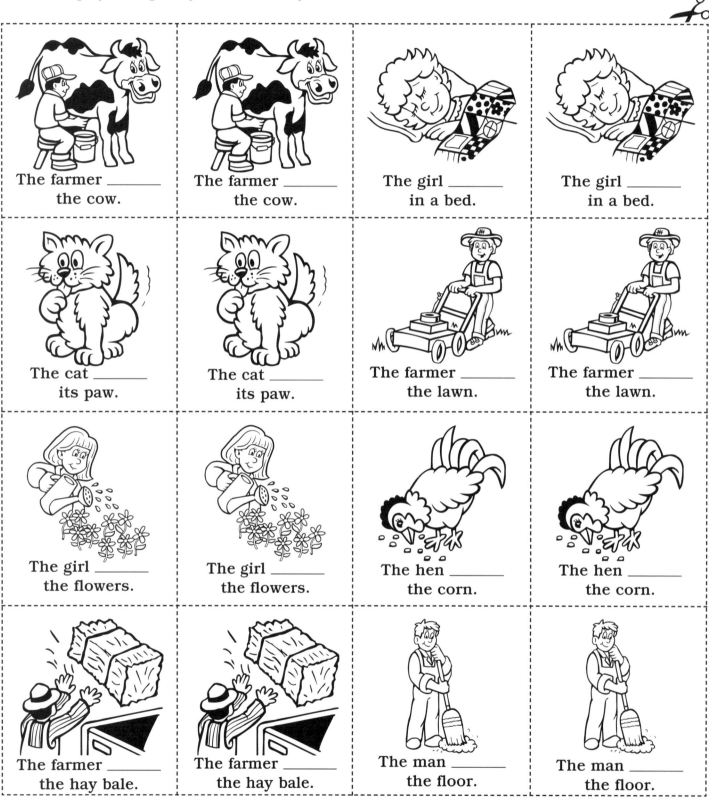

Homework Partner   Date

Game Board 5

Third Person Present Tense

Corn in the Bushel

Directions: Cut out the ears of corn at the bottom of the page along the dotted lines. Cut the slot at the top of the bushel of corn. Pick a word and use it in a sentence with a person or animal. (The **farmer chops** the wood.) Then, place the corn in the slot at the top of the bushel.

chops | drinks | barks | plants | feeds | eats | picks

Homework Partner   Date

Game Board 5

Third Person Present Tense

Third Person Verb Tic-Tac-Toe

Directions: Cut out the Tic-Tac-Toe tokens below. One player gets the "**sheep**" and the other gets the "**cows**." Player one picks out a square, reads and completes the sentence with the appropriate third person present tense verb. (The hen **pecks** the corn.) Player one puts a token on the picture. Second player follows in turn. Three in a row wins.

Homework Partner   Date

Game Board 5

Third Person Present Tense

Third Person Present Tense Spinner Activity

Directions: If you prefer, glue this page to construction paper for added durability. Cut out the arrow/dial. Use a brad to connect the dial to the circle. Spin the spinner. Say each sentence using the correct present tense verb. (The farmer **picks** the corn.)

Game Board 5
Third Person Present Tense

Third Person Present Tense Puzzle

Directions: Cut out and shuffle the puzzle pieces on page 79 and place them face up. Pick a puzzle piece and read the present tense verb. (The farmer **picks** the corn.) Then, find the picture and sentence on this page that correspond to the verb on the puzzle piece. Place the puzzle piece on the puzzle. Then, say the sentence.

The farmer _____ the corn.

The pig _____ in the mud.

The girl _____ the horse.

The man _____ a hole.

The farmer _____ the field.

The man _____ the water.

The girl _____ the leaves.

The farmer _____ the cow.

The girl _____ in a bed.

The cat _____ its paw.

The girl _____ the flowers.

The dog _____ at the cat.

Homework Partner

Date

Game Board 5

Third Person Present Tense

Third Person Present Tense Puzzle

Directions: Cut out and shuffle the puzzle pieces below. Then, follow the instructions on page 78.

picks	plays	rides
digs	plows	pours
rakes	milks	sleeps
licks	waters	barks

Homework Partner   Date

Game Board 5

Third Person Present Tense

Color a Can

Directions: Fill in the blank in each sentence with an appropriate present tense verb. (The farmer **picks** the corn.) Color each milk can as you go.

The man ___ the floor.

The rooster ___ at dawn.

The horse ___ the water.

The cat ___ its paw.

The man ___ the grass.

The farmer ___ the corn.

The girl ___ the horse.

The man ___ a hole.

--- Word Bank ---

| digs | sweeps | licks | mows |
| rides | crows | picks | drinks |

Homework Partner   Date

Game Board 5

Third Person Present Tense

Color the Correct Chicken

Directions: Listen to or read each sentence below. Color in the chicken that correctly completes each sentence. Then, read each sentence correctly. _____

1. The hen  the corn.

2. The girl  the flowers.

3. The man 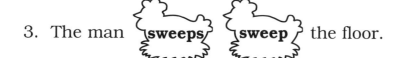 the floor.

4. The farmer  the grass.

5. The girl  in a bed.

6. Farmer Fred  an apple.

7. The horse  water.

8. The farmer  the hay.

9. The rooster  at dawn.

10. The cat  its paws.

_____   _____
Homework Partner   Date

Game Board 5

Third Person Present Tense

Third Person Present Tense Crossword

Directions: Fill in the blanks in the sentences below. Then, complete the crossword puzzle.

Answer Key: DOWN 1. digs, 3. sweeps, 4. rakes, 6. feeds ACROSS 2. milks, 4. rides, 5. eats, 7. sleeps

Down

1. The farmer _____ a hole with a shovel.
3. The man _____ the floor with a broom.
4. In the fall, the girl _____ the leaves.
6. When the animals are hungry, the farmer _____ them.
2. The farmer _____ the cow.

Across

4. The girl puts a saddle on the horse when she _____ it.
5. The horse _____ hay and oats.
7. The girl _____ in a bed.

Word Bank

| feeds | sweeps | digs | sleeps |
| eats | rakes | milks | rides |

Homework Partner _____ Date _____

Game Board 5
Third Person Present Tense

82 #BK-298 "Say and Do"® Grammar Game Boards Fun Sheets • ©2002 Super Duper® Publications • www.superduperinc.com

Add a Patch

Directions: Color Farmer Freida and the patches at the bottom of the page. Cut out the patches. Choose a patch, use the word in a sentence, and glue/tape or place it on Farmer Freida's shirt and hat.

| waters | licks | milks | pours | digs | plays |
| eats | feeds | barks | drinks | chops | sweeps |

Homework Partner   Date

Third Person Present Tense

Help Farmer Freida Stack-Em-Up

Directions: Cut out the feed sacks at the bottom of the page. Choose a sack, say a sentence about the picture using the present tense verb on the sack. (The man **smells** the flowers.) Then, glue/tape or place the sack in the barn.

pets fills stacks smells rolls

jumps opens rings pulls

Homework Partner   Date

Third Person Present Tense

Roll-a-Verb

Directions: Assemble the cube as follows: Glue onto construction paper for added durability. Cut along the dotted lines. Fold on solid lines and glue as indicated. To play: roll the cube. Say a sentence about the picture on the top side of the cube. Remember to use a third person present tense verb in your sentence. (The man **smells** the flower.) Keep rolling the cube until you have a sentence for all six pictures.

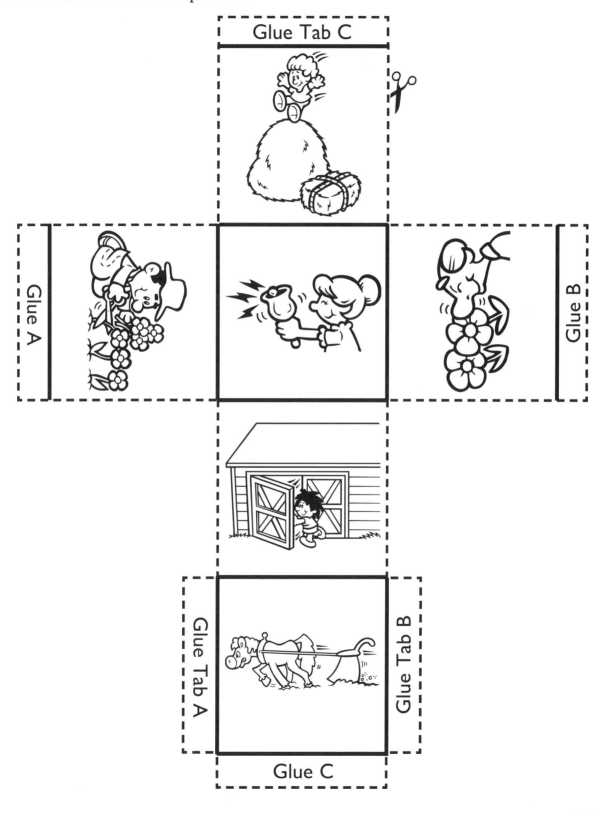

Homework Partner   Date

Third Person Present Tense

#BK-298 "Say and Do" ® Grammar Game Boards Fun Sheets • ©2002 Super Duper® Publications • www.superduperinc.com

85

Present Tense Farm Scene

Directions: Circle the picture showing the following verbs: **pets**, **jumps**, **opens**, **rolls**, **stacks**, and **pulls**. As you circle each verb, say a sentence using that verb. (The boy **pets** the horse.)

Third Person Present Tense

_____ _____
Homework Partner   Date

86 #BK-298 "Say and Do" ® Grammar Game Boards Fun Sheets • ©2002 Super Duper® Publications • www.superduperinc.com

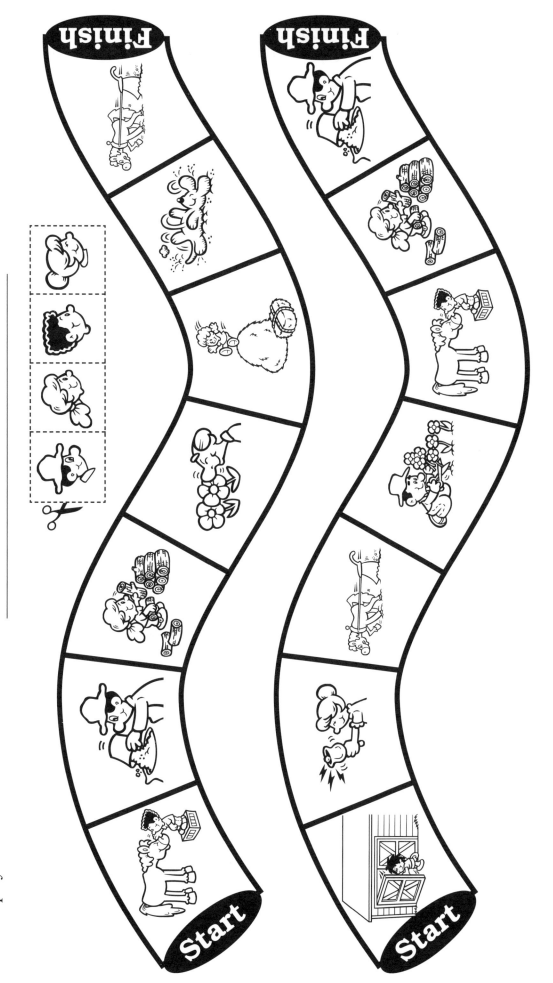

Plow the Field Race

Directions: Cut out the game markers below. Each player chooses a field and places a game marker on the "start." Flip a coin to determine the number of spaces to move. Heads, move one space. Tails, move two spaces. Take turns plowing the fields. For each picture you land on say a sentence using the third person present tense. (The man **smells** the flower.) The first player to reach the finish line wins.

Homework Partner

Date

Third Person Present Tense

Happy Piggy – Sad Piggy

Directions: Read each sentence. If the sentence is correct, color the happy pig. If the sentence is incorrect, color the sad pig.

1. The boy pets the horse.

2. Farmer Fred fills his sack.

3. The girl stack the wood.

4. The man smells the flower.

5. The boy jump in the hay.

6. The dog roll in the dirt.

7. The horse pulls the plow.

8. The girl open the barn door.

9. Mom ring the lunch bell.

10. The farmer cuts the flowers.

Homework Partner   Date

Third Person Present Tense

What's Missing?

Directions: Look at each picture. Something is missing. Tell what is missing and say a sentence for each picture using a third person present tense verb. (The farmer **cuts** the flowers.) _____

Homework Partner   Date

Third Person Present Tense

Fun on the Farm

Directions: Read the story. Fill in each blank with the correct verb.

Jack and Jane love to visit Grandpa's farm. Jack _____ (pet, pets) Trotter, the horse, as soon as they arrive. Trotter _____ (pull, pulls) Grandpa's plow. Jane _____ (open, opens) the barn door. Ruff, Grandpa's dog, _____ (come, comes) to greet her. Ruff loves to _____ (roll, rolls) in the dirt. He is so playful! Grandpa _____ (come, comes) out to see Jack and Jane. Grandpa does many jobs on the farm. He _____ (stack, stacks) the firewood and _____ (fill, fills) all the feed sacks with corn. Grandma _____ (cut, cuts) the flowers. Jane _____ (smell, smells) them. They smell so good! Jack and Jane love to _____ (jump, jumps) in the hay. The farm is such a fun place to visit!

_____   _____
Homework Partner   Date

Third Person Present Tense

Is/Are Tic-Tac-Toe

Directions: Cut out the Tic-Tac-Toe tokens below. One player gets "**seesaws**" and the other gets "**slides**." The first player picks out a square, inserts either "**is**" or "**are**" in the sentence and puts a token on the picture. The second player follows in turn. Three in a row wins.

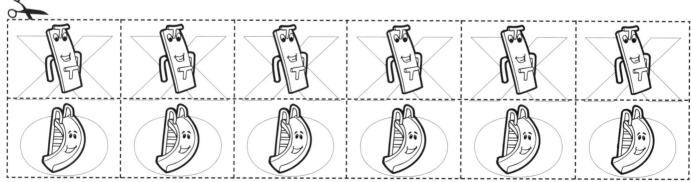

Homework Partner   Date

Game Board 6
Is and Are

Is/Are Memory Game

Directions: If you prefer, glue this page onto construction paper for added durability. Cut out all of the cards and place them face down on the table. Player one turns over a card and says/reads the sentence, inserting "**is**" or "**are**" as appropriate. The player then turns over a second card, saying the sentence. The player keeps any matches. Play continues in turn. Most matches win.

Homework Partner   Date

Game Board 6
Is and Are

Is or Are Puzzle

Directions: Cut out and shuffle the puzzle pieces on page 95 and place them face up. Pick a puzzle piece and say either the "**is**" or "**are**" sentence about the picture. (The boy **is** sliding down the slide.) Then, match the picture to the correct sentence on this page. Place the puzzle piece on the puzzle. Then, say the sentence.

- The boy _____ sliding down the slide.
- The girls _____ jumping rope.
- The girl _____ throwing a baseball.
- The boys _____ swinging.
- The girl _____ licking a lollipop.
- The boy _____ running.
- The girls _____ playing hopscotch.
- The girl _____ pushing the carriage.
- The girl _____ feeding the duck.
- The boy _____ falling down.
- The boys _____ blowing bubbles.
- The girl _____ blowing a whistle.

Game Board 6
Is and Are

Puzzle Fun

Directions: Cut out and shuffle the puzzle pieces below. Then, follow the instructions on page 94.

Homework Partner   Date

Game Board 6
Is and Are

95

Is/Are Match Up

Directions: If you prefer, glue this page to construction paper for added durability. Cut out the picture–cards below along the dotted lines. Pick a picture-card and say the sentence using "is" or "are." (He **is** playing./They **are** swinging.) Glue/tape or place picture on the appropriate sand toy.

Homework Partner   Date

Game Board 6
Is and Are

Is/Are Fun on the Monkey Bars

Directions: Look at the pictures on the monkey bars. Say a sentence about each picture using either **"is"** or **"are."** (They **are** swinging./He **is** sliding.) Color each rung as you go.

Game Board 6
Is and Are

Homework Partner _____   Date _____

Is/Are Spinner Activity

Directions: If you prefer, glue this page to construction paper for added durability. Cut out the arrow/dial. Use a brad to connect the dial to the circle. Spin the spinner. Say each sentence using either "**is**" or "**are**." Take turns with your speech helper.

Homework Partner   Date

Game Board 6
Is and Are

Listening for Is or Are

Directions: Read each sentence. If the sentence correctly uses "**is**" or "**are**," color the smiling sun. If the sentence does not correctly use "**is**" or "**are**," color the frowning sun.

1. The children **are** reading.

2. The children **is** eating.

3. The boy **are** drinking.

4. The children **are** building a sandcastle.

5. The girl **is** hiding.

6. The children **are** climbing.

7. The girl **are** walking.

8. The boy **is** sliding.

9. The girls **is** jumping rope.

10. The girl **is** throwing a baseball.

Homework Partner   Date

Game Board 6
Is and Are

Is/Are Ice Cream Cones

Directions: Read each sentence below and choose either "**is**" or "**are**" to complete each sentence. Color the correct word.

1. The boys   swinging.

2. The girl   licking a lollipop.

3. The girl   pushing a carriage.

4. The boy   falling down.

5. The boys   blowing bubbles.

6. The children   playing jacks.

7. The girl   rollerblading.

8. The children   hugging.

_____ _____
Homework Partner   Date

Game Board 6
Is and Are

Fill in Is or Are

Directions: As you read the story below, fill in each blank with "**is**" or "**are**."

Where is Katie?

It is such a beautiful day. I am going to meet my friend, Katie, at the playground. I think I will look for Katie by the swings. Two boys _____ swinging, but I don't see Katie. Maybe she _____ playing hopscotch. Two little girls _____ playing hopscotch, but not Katie. Zoooom! That boy _____ running so fast! I wonder if he saw Katie? Where could she be? I see my friend Judy. Judy _____ sitting on the bench. "Hi, Judy! Did you see Katie?" "No, I didn't," said Judy, "Maybe she _____ climbing on the monkey bars." "Thanks. I'll go there and look!" A boy and a girl _____ climbing, but not Katie. Look! Someone _____ hiding behind the tree. Guess who _____ hiding behind the tree? It's Katie! Katie _____ hiding behind the tree!

Homework Partner

Date

Game Board 6

Is and Are

Is/Are Scene

Directions: Look for the following things in the scene below: boys blowing bubbles; girl licking a lollipop; boy running; boys swinging; girl hiding; and girls playing hopscotch. Circle each one and tell what he, she, or they are doing. Don't forget to use "**is**" or "**are**" in your sentence. (He **is** running./They **are** swinging.)

Homework Partner _____ Date _____

Sliding with Is/Are

Directions: As you go up the slide, say a sentence about each picture using either "**is**" or "**are**." Color the picture when you are at the top of the slide.

Homework Partner   Date   Is and Are

Shoot for the Hoop

Directions: Cut out the basketballs below. Cut the slot at the top of each basketball hoop. Choose a basketball and say a sentence for each picture using "**is**" or "**are**." (They **are** clapping./She **is** jumping.) Place the basketball in the correct hoop. Keep playing until you have made a "basket" with each ball.

Homework Partner   Date   Is and Are

Yummy Popsicle Fun

Directions: Read the sentence on the left side of each popsicle. Which word is missing, "**is**" or "**are**"? Write the word "**is**" or "**are**" on the right side of the popsicle to correctly complete the sentence. Color the popsicles.

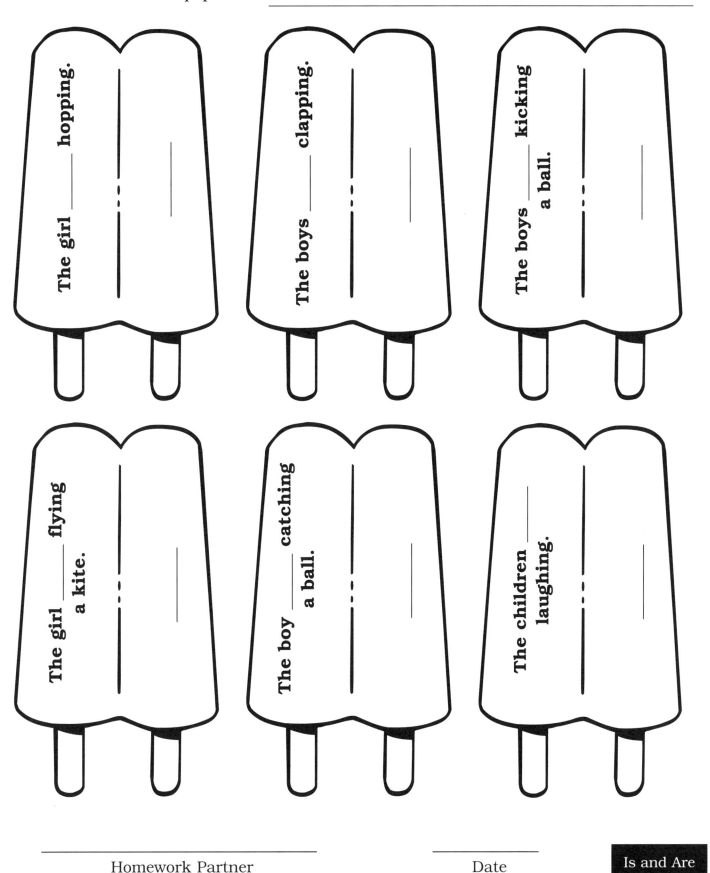

Homework Partner   Date

Is and Are

Drop-a-Penny

Directions: Take a penny and hold it above this worksheet. Drop the penny onto the worksheet. Make up a sentence about the picture under the penny. Don't forget to use "**is**" or "**are**" in your sentence. (He **is** holding the box./They **are** clapping.) Take turns with your speech helper.

Homework Partner   Date   Is and Are

Silly Scene

Directions: Look at the scene below. Can you find six silly things? Circle each silly thing and tell what is happening. Don't forget to use "**is**" or "**are**" in your sentence.

Is and Are

Date _____

Homework Partner _____

107

Is/Are Cut and Paste

Directions: Cut out the "**is**" and "**are**" cards at the bottom of the page along the dotted lines. Read the sentence next to each picture. Choose the correct word, "**is**" or "**are**," to complete each sentence. Glue/tape or place the correct word in the blank.

	The boys ☐ kicking the ball.		The girl ☐ pulling a wagon.
	The boy ☐ catching a ball.		The girls ☐ hanging from the bars.
	The boys ☐ clapping.		The boy ☐ spinning a top.
	The girl ☐ flying a kite.		The children ☐ holding hands.

| is | is | is | is | are | are | are | are |

Homework Partner   Date   Is and Are

Circus Tense

Regular Past Tense Verbs

Game Board 7

Grammar Game Board

Fun Sheets

Regular Past Tense Tic-Tac-Toe

Directions: Cut out the Tic-Tac-Toe tokens below. One player gets "**zebras**" and the other gets "**elephants**." As you cover each square, add the correct ending to make each verb past tense. Say it in a sentence. (Yesterday, the girl **watched** the show.) The second player follows in turn. Three in a row wins.

Homework Partner   Date

Game Board 7

Regular Past Tense Verbs

Popcorn Time

Directions: On each popcorn container you will see three words that are associated with one of the verbs on a piece of popcorn. Read the three words and choose the verb that best fits with all three items. Write that verb on the line at the top of each popcorn container.

Homework Partner Date

Game Board 7
Regular Past Tense Verbs

Sentence Completion

Directions: Read each sentence. Fill in the blank with the verb pictured below it. You can also use these cards to play sentence/picture memory.

The boy _____ on the tightrope. 	The children _____. 	The lion _____. 	The girl _____ the balls. 	The children _____ at the clown. 
The puppy _____ through the hoop. 	The girl _____ on the mat. 	The vendor _____ the popcorn. 	The ringmaster _____ to the elephant. 	The monkey _____ the horn. 

Word Bank

| jumped | popped | laughed | cheered | flipped |
| roared | pointed | walked | honked | juggled |

Homework Partner   Date

Game Board 7
Regular Past Tense Verbs

Peanuts for Penelope

Directions: Cut out the peanuts at the bottom of the page. Then, cut out the space in Penelope's mouth. Say each verb in a sentence as you feed the peanuts to Penelope. (The girl **juggled** the balls.)

| juggled | jumped | danced | balanced | cheered |
| laughed | watched | climbed | honked | pointed |

Game Board 7
Regular Past Tense Verbs

Spinner Game

Directions: If you prefer, glue this page to construction paper for added durability. Cut out the arrow/dial. Use a brad to connect the dial to the circle. Spin the spinner. To play, take turns spinning the spinner and describing the picture using a regular past tense verb.

Game Board 7
Regular Past Tense Verbs

Come to the Big Top Circus

Directions: Read each sentence. Then, complete each sentence using one of the verbs on the Big Top tent. Color the tent when you are finished.

Verbs on tent: walked, roared, honked, pointed, climbed, laughed, balanced, watched, cheered, juggled, smiled, flipped

1. The girl _____ a plate on her nose.
2. The little boy _____ from ear to ear.
3. The ringmaster _____ at the trapeze artist.
4. The kids _____ the lions perform.
5. The children _____ at the funny clown.
6. The lions _____ at the lion tamer.
7. The kids _____ up the stairs.
8. The crowd _____ , "Hooray!"
9. The acrobat _____ upside down.
10. The juggler _____ the balls.
11. The monkey _____ the horn.
12. The girl _____ the ladder.

Homework Partner _____   Date _____

Game Board 7
Regular Past Tense Verbs

Circus Scene

Directions: Cut out and glue/tape or place the animals around the scene. Read each present tense verb and change it to the past tense by adding "d" or "ed" (**bark-barked**). Then, say each past tense verb in a sentence. (The lion **roared**.)

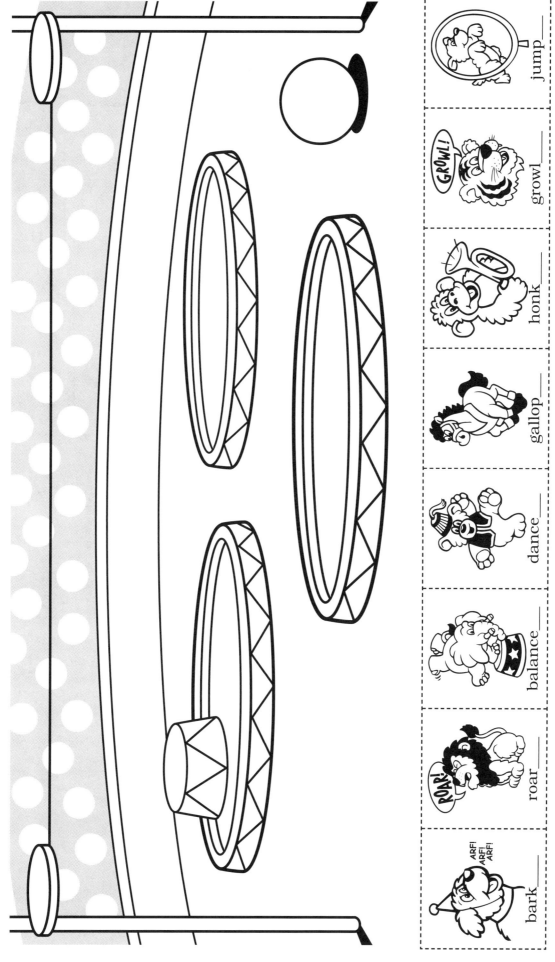

Game Board 7
Regular Past Tense Verbs

Homework Partner _____ Date _____

Follow the Circus Path

Directions: Help the kids find their way to the circus tent! Say each word along the way, adding the past tense ending to each word. Then, use the word in a sentence. (The lion **roared**.)

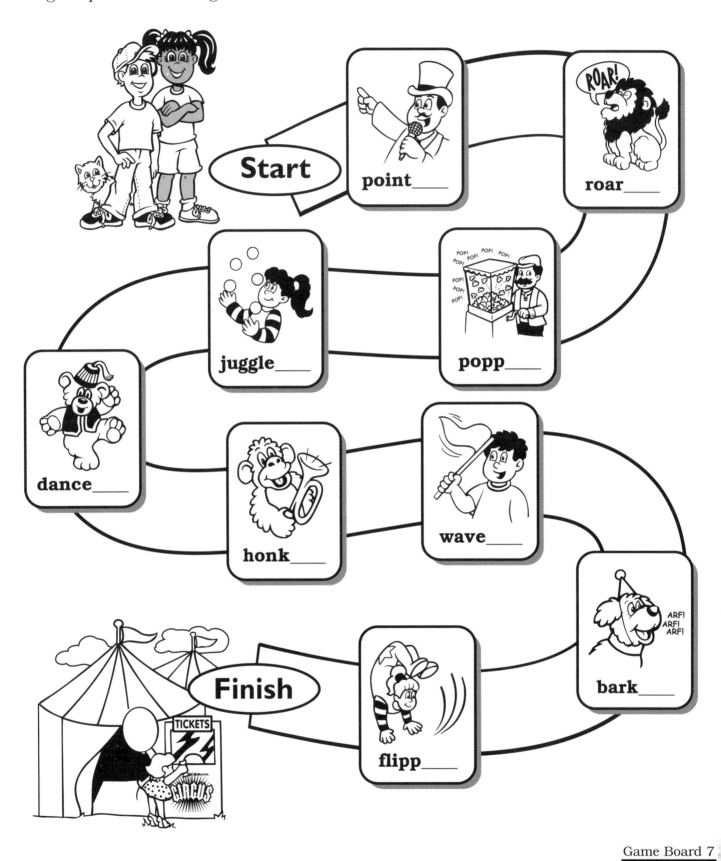

Homework Partner   Date

Game Board 7
Regular Past Tense Verbs

Memory

Directions: If you prefer, glue this page to construction paper for added durability. Change each word to past tense by adding "**d**" or "**ed**." Cut out all the cards and place them face down on the table. Player one flips two cards, trying to match a word card with a corresponding past tense picture card. Say the past tense verb in a sentence. (The flag **waved**.) Play continues in turn. The player with the most matches wins!

walk___	popp___	pedal___	jump___
honk___	wave___	bark___	dance___

_____ Homework Partner   _____ Date

Game Board 7

Regular Past Tense Verbs

Circus Charades

Directions: Glue this page to construction paper for added durability. Cut out all the cards and place them face down on the table. Take turns choosing a card. Without showing your card to the other players, act out the picture. See if the other players can guess what you are doing!

 The girl **giggled**.	 The boy **picked** a balloon.	 The lion tamer **tamed** the lion.
 The boy **licked** a lollipop.	 The audience **clapped**.	 The boy **spilled** the popcorn.
 The vendor **filled** the bag with popcorn.	 The clown **dressed** for the circus.	 The lion tamer **cracked** his whip.
 The clown **winked** at the children.	 The monkeys **played** with a ball.	 The strong man **lifted** 1000 lbs.

Homework Partner   Date

Color the Juggler's Plates

Directions: Choose a picture on one of the plates. Add the ending to the word to form the past tense. Use the past tense word in a sentence. (The children **clapped**.) Color the plate.

Regular Past Tense Verbs

Date _____

Homework Partner _____

Listening for Past Tense

Directions: Read each sentence. If the sentence correctly uses the verb tense, color the smiling clown. If the sentence does not correctly use the verb tense, color the frowning clown.

1. Yesterday, the audience **clapped**.

2. The girl **giggled** tomorrow.

3. The boy **lick** a lollipop.

4. The lion tamer **tamed** the lion.

5. The clown **wink** last week.

6. The boy **spilled** his popcorn.

7. The strong man **lifted** one thousand pounds.

8. The boy **pick** a balloon.

Homework Partner   Date

Make a Clown

Directions: Color and cut out the clown pieces below. Attach the head and leg pieces to the body using three brads. Once your clown is assembled, tell _____ things your clown did using the past tense. (My clown **juggled** three balls. My clown **smiled** at me, etc.) _____

Homework Partner   Date

Regular Past Tense Verbs

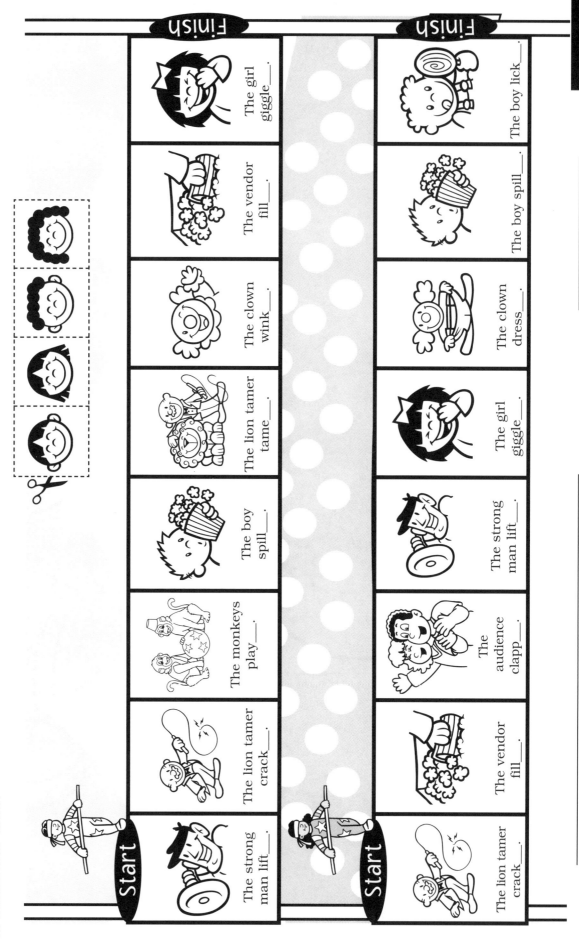

Circus Flags Cut and Paste

Directions: Cut out all the flags at the bottom of the page. Match each picture to a word on a flag and glue/tape or place it on top. Use each word in a sentence. (I **spilled** milk.)

_____ _____
Homework Partner   Date

Regular Past Tense Verbs

Circus Crossword

Directions: Look at each sentence and complete the crossword below using past tense verbs. Use the pictures around the puzzle for clues.

Answer Key: DOWN 1. cracked, 2. filled, 5. spilled ACROSS 3. picked, 4. clapped, 6. winked, 7. played

DOWN

1. The lion tamer _____ his whip.
2. The vendor _____ the bags of popcorn.
5. The boy _____ a balloon.

ACROSS

3. The boy _____ his popcorn.
4. The audience _____.
6. The clown _____ at the children.
7. The monkeys _____ with a ball.

Homework Partner

Date

Regular Past Tense Verbs

Hard Hat Fun

Directions: Cut out the hard hats at the bottom of the page. Look at each picture and choose the correct past tense verb from the hard hats. Glue/tape or place each hard hat onto a worker's head. Use each past tense verb in a sentence. (She **wore** a hard hat.)

Game Board 8
Irregular Past Tense

Irregular Past Tense Tic-Tac-Toe

Directions: Cut out the Tic-Tac-Toe tokens below. One player gets the "**hammers**" and the other gets the "**wrenches.**" Player one picks out a square, reads and completes the sentence with the appropriate irregular past tense verb. Player one puts a token on the picture. Second player follows in turn. Three in a row wins.

Homework Partner   Date

Game Board 8

Irregular Past Tense

Irregular Past Tense Spinner Activity

Directions: If you prefer, glue this page to construction paper for added durability. Cut out the arrow/dial. Use a brad to connect the dial to the circle. Spin the spinner. Say each sentence using the correct irregular past tense verb.

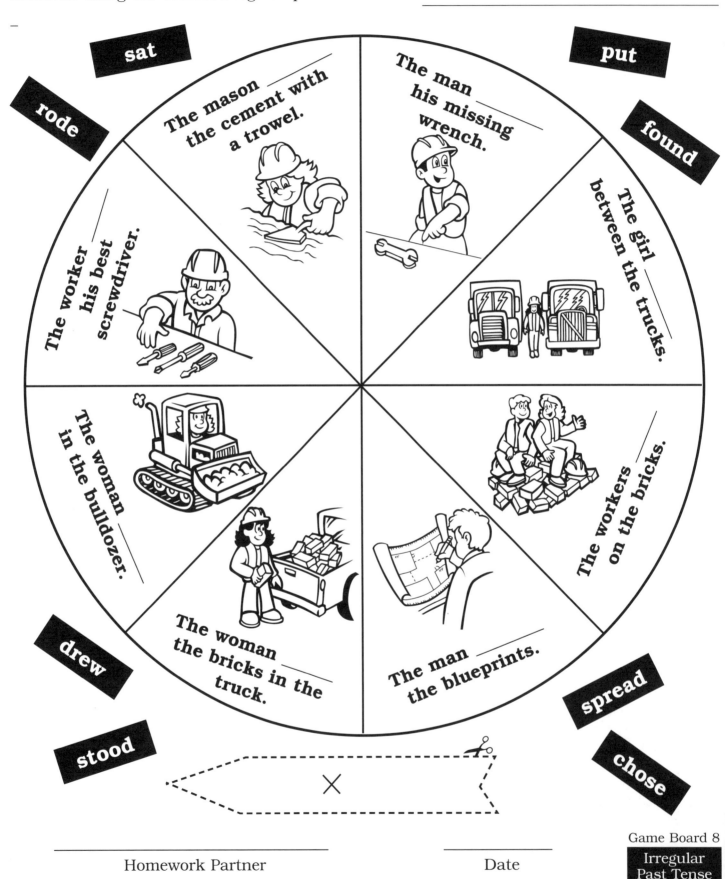

Homework Partner _____ Date _____

Game Board 8
Irregular Past Tense

Memory for Irregular Past Tense

Directions: If you prefer, glue this page onto construction paper for added durability. Cut out all of the cards and place them face down on the table. Player one turns over a card and changes the verb to past tense to complete the sentence. The player then turns over a second card trying to find its match. Keep all matches. Play continues in turn. Most matches win.

Yesterday, Mr. Jones (hit) _____ the nail.

Yesterday, Mr. Jones (hit) _____ the nail.

Yesterday, Sam (hurt) _____ his thumb.

Yesterday, Sam (hurt) _____ his thumb.

Yesterday, Joe (dig) _____ a hole.

Yesterday, Joe (dig) _____ a hole.

Yesterday, Sue (stand) _____ between the trucks.

Yesterday, Sue (stand) _____ between the trucks.

Yesterday, the workers (sit) _____ on the bricks.

Yesterday, the workers (sit) _____ on the bricks.

Yesterday, Mike (draw) _____ the plans.

Yesterday, Mike (draw) _____ the plans.

Yesterday, Bill (break) _____ the hammer.

Yesterday, Bill (break) _____ the hammer.

Yesterday, Joan (throw) _____ the bricks in the truck.

Yesterday, Joan (throw) _____ the bricks in the truck.

_____ _____ Game Board 8
Homework Partner   Date   Irregular Past Tense

#BK-298 Grammar Game Board Fun Sheets • ©2002 Super Duper® Publications • 1-800-277-8737 • Online! www.superduperinc.com   131

Find the Hammer

Directions: If you prefer, glue this page onto construction paper for added durability. Cut out all the cards and place them face down in a pile. Take turns flipping the top card on the pile and saying a sentence about the picture using an irregular past tense verb. (Yesterday, she **drove** the truck.) The person who turns over the hammer wins! Shuffle the deck and play again.

Homework Partner   Date

Game Board 8
Irregular Past Tense

Make Your Own Bulldozer

Directions: If you prefer, glue this page to construction paper for added durability. Cut out the bulldozer, shovel, and word strip. Cut the two dotted lines on the side of the bulldozer and insert the word strip. Pull the word strip to expose a word. Use the word in a sentence. (I **found** a penny.) Repeat this activity for all six verbs. _____

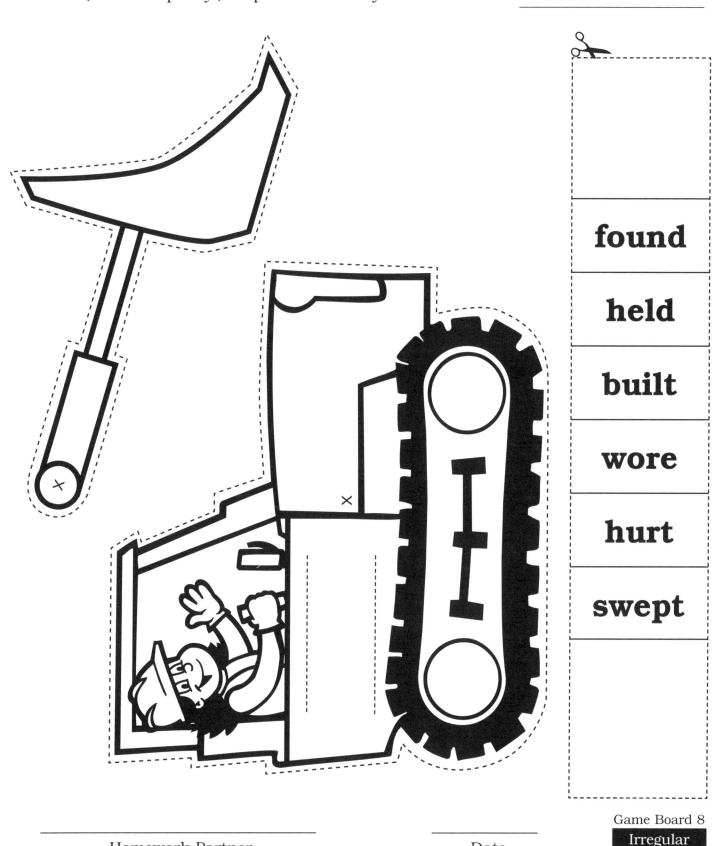

Homework Partner   Date

Game Board 8
Irregular Past Tense

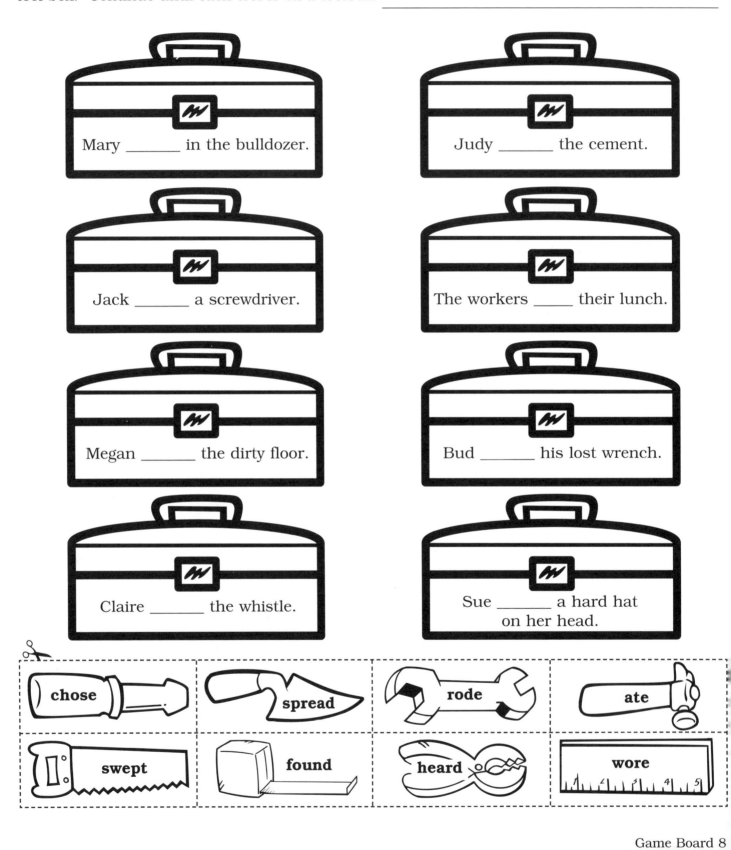

Help Trudy Build a Wall

Directions: Color the cards below red. Cut out the cards along the dotted lines. Pick a word–card and use it in a sentence. (Yesterday, I **rode** my bike.) Glue/tape or place each word–card beside Trudy and build the wall. Continue until all cards have been used. Don't forget to say a sentence for each one!

spread	chose	rode	put	broke	drew
sat	stood	found	drank	swept	bent
dug	hurt	held	hit	lost	fell

Homework Partner

Date

Game Board 8

Irregular Past Tense

Color the End of the Wrench

Directions: Read each sentence on the wrench. Choose the word that correctly completes each sentence. Color the correct end of the wrench.

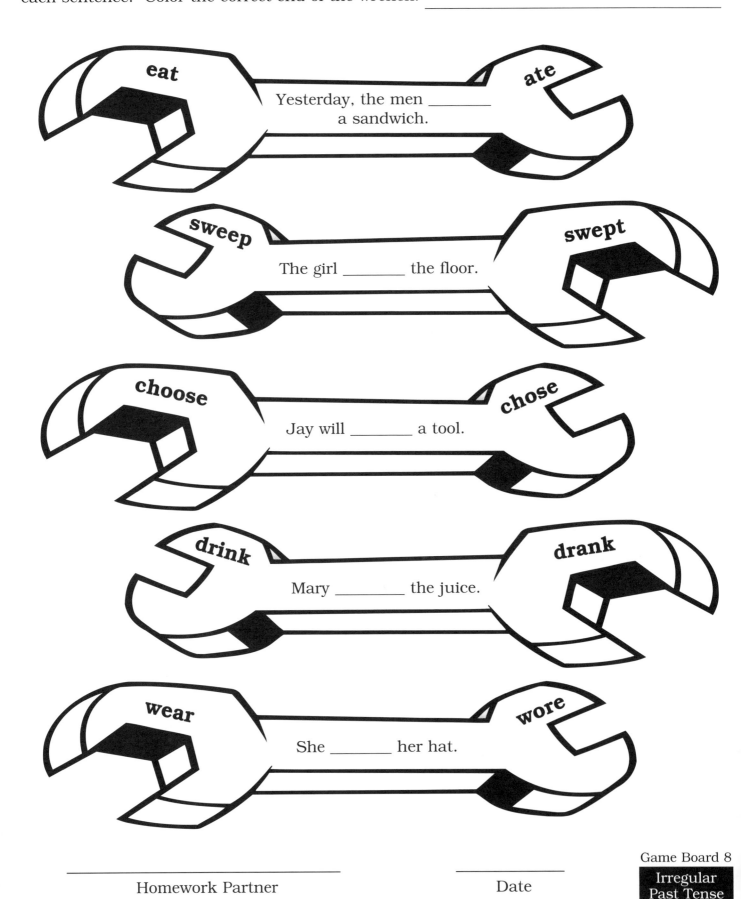

Game Board 8
Irregular Past Tense

Past or Present Spinner Activity

Directions: If you prefer, glue this page to construction paper for added durability. Cut out the arrows and spinners below. Use a brad to connect the arrows to the spinners. Spin both spinners. Spinner one tells you if your sentence will be in the past tense (yesterday) or present (now). Spinner two tells you what verb to use. Complete the sentence using the words indicated on the spinners. (Remember to change the verb to make it agree with the past or present tense of the sentence.)

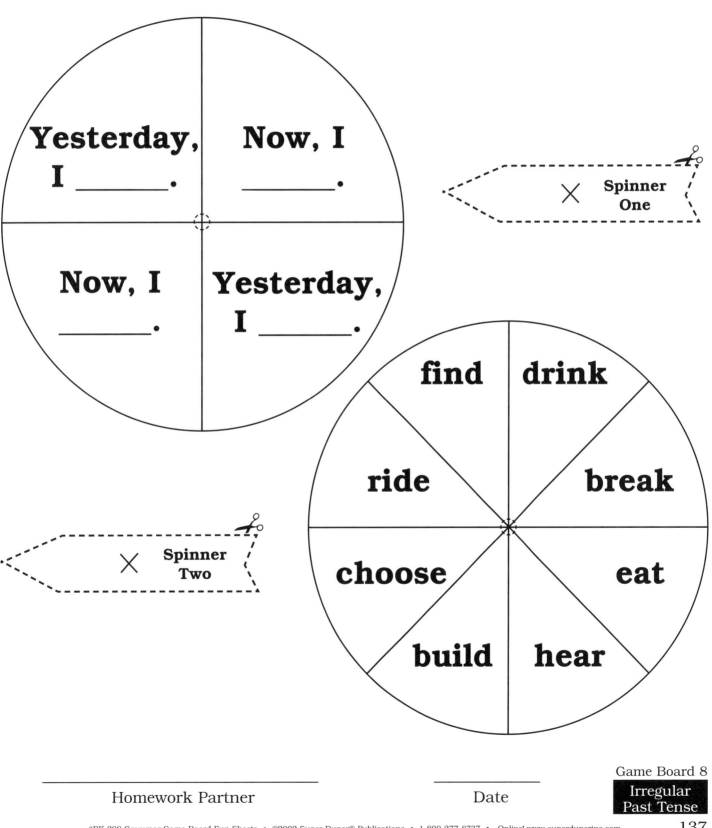

Homework Partner _____   Date _____

Game Board 8
Irregular Past Tense

Construction Word Search

Directions: Read each sentence. Change each verb to the irregular past tense and write it in the blank. Then, find each verb in the puzzle.

T	A	R	L	T	C	S	D
O	T	H	O	U	G	H	T
F	B	K	I	J	A	O	H
V	C	U	T	O	V	O	R
A	W	O	R	L	E	K	E
N	N	B	L	E	W	O	W

Answer key: p.216

Sally _____ the rope to Pete.
(throw)

Al _____ the wood with a saw.
(cut)

The whistle _____ at lunch time.
(blow)

Bill _____ about the new house.
(think)

The workers _____ hands.
(shake)

Joe _____ the plan to Mike.
(give)

Homework Partner   Date

Irregular Past Tense

Circle a Word

Directions: Read each sentence below. Circle the correct verb to complete the sentence.

1. Mary _____ (**bite, bit**) into the sandwich.

2. Charlie _____ (**ran, run**) after the truck.

3. Dina will _____ (**sink, sank**) in the mud.

4. Sally _____ (**throw, threw**) the rope.

5. Yesterday, the men _____ (**shake, shook**) hands.

6. Fran _____ (**make, made**) a wall.

7. Jim _____ (**saw, see**) his friend.

8. Joe will _____ (**give, gave**) the plans to Mike.

9. The man will _____ (**think, thought**) about his new house.

10. The whistle _____ (**blow, blew**).

_____   _____
Homework Partner   Date

Irregular Past Tense

Irregular Past Tense Puzzle

Directions: Cut out and shuffle the puzzle pieces on page 141 and place face up. Pick a puzzle piece and say the word. Look at the pictures and sentences on this page. Find the picture and sentence that correspond to that irregular past tense verb. Place the puzzle piece on the puzzle. Then, say the sentence. (Jim **saw** his friend.)

Jim _____ his friend.

Joe _____ the plans to Mike.

Bill _____ about the new house.

Dina _____ in the mud.

The whistle _____.

Jay _____ the bag of cement.

Al _____ wood with a saw.

Mary _____ a sandwich.

Charlie _____ after the truck.

Sally _____ the rope to Pete.

The workers _____ hands.

Fran _____ a brick wall.

Game Board 8
Irregular Past Tense

Puzzle Fun

Instructions: Cut out and shuffle the puzzle pieces below. Then, follow the instructions on page 140.

saw	gave	thought
sank	blew	caught
cut	bit	ran
threw	shook	made

Homework Partner   Date

Irregular Past Tense

Irregular Past Tense Maze

Directions: Can you help the construction worker find his toolbox? As you follow the maze, say a sentence using the irregular past tense verb for each picture you pass. (He **ran** after the truck.)

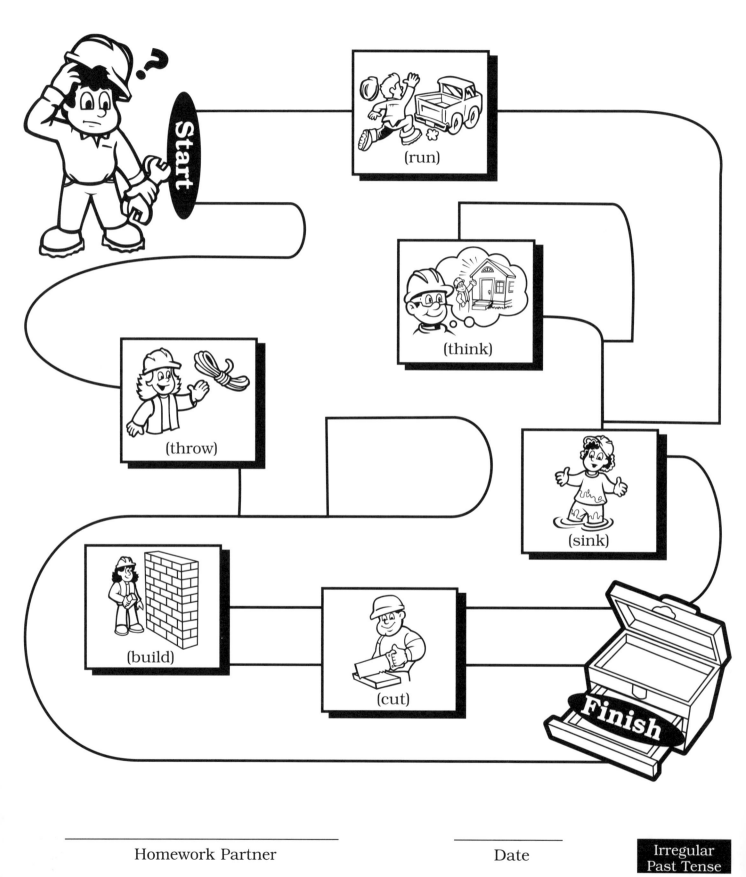

Homework Partner Date

Irregular Past Tense

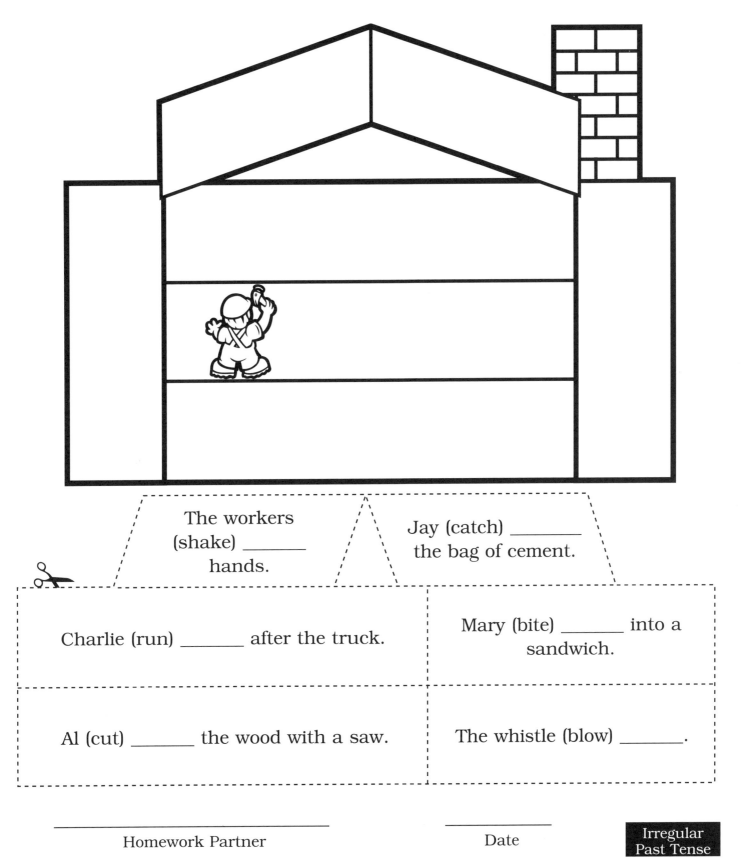

Irregular Verb Match

Directions: Look at the picture on the left of the page. Draw a line to connect the picture to the correct verb on the right side of the page. Say a sentence for each picture. (The worker **sank** in the mud.)

sat

sank

gave

made

shook

caught

Homework Partner   Date

Irregular Past Tense

Sports Talk Memory Game

Directions: If you prefer, glue this page onto construction paper for added durability. Cut out all of the cards and place them face down on the table. Player one turns over a card and says/reads the sentence, inserting "**has**" or "**have**" as appropriate. (The boy **has** a golf club.) Player then turns over a second card, saying the sentence. Keep any matches. Play continues in turn. Most matches wins!

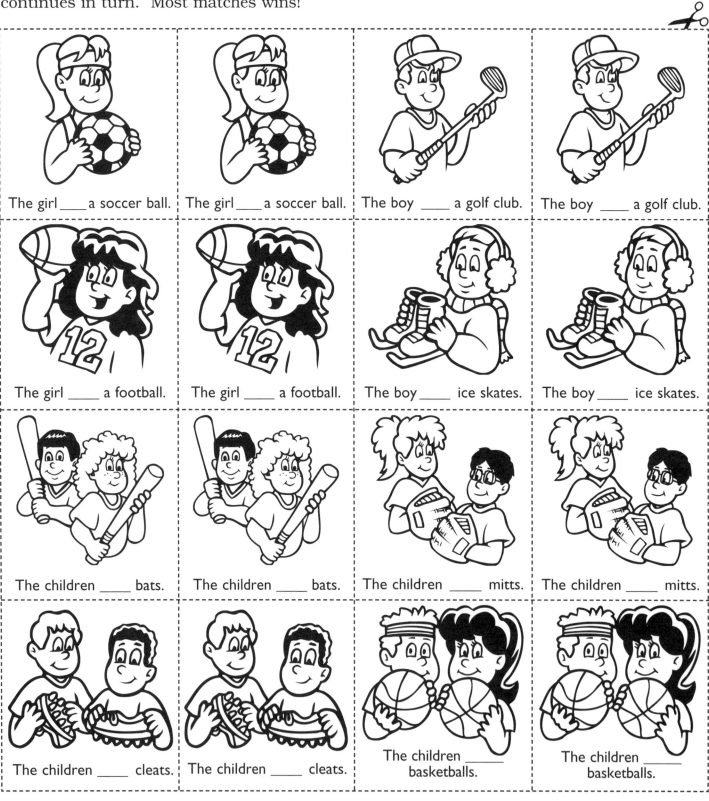

Homework Partner   Date

Game Board 9

Has/Have

Sports Man

Directions: Sports Man loves sports. He has a lot of sports equipment. Name each item he has and say it in a "**has**" sentence. (He **has** a football.)

Homework Partner   Date

Game Board 9
Has/Have

Sports Talk Spinner

Directions: If you prefer, glue this page to construction paper for added durability. Cut out the arrow/dial. Use a brad to connect the dial to the circle. Spin the spinner and use the word indicated on the spinner to complete a sentence under one of the pictures on the page. (The girl **has** a softball.) Continue until you have read all the sentences.

Homework Partner   Date

Game Board 9
Has/Have

Have/Has Tic-Tac-Toe

Directions: Cut out the Tic-Tac-Toe tokens below. One player gets "**baseballs**" and the other gets the "**footballs**." Player one picks out a square, reads and completes the sentence with "have" or "has." Player one puts a token on the picture. Second player follows in turn. Three in a row wins.

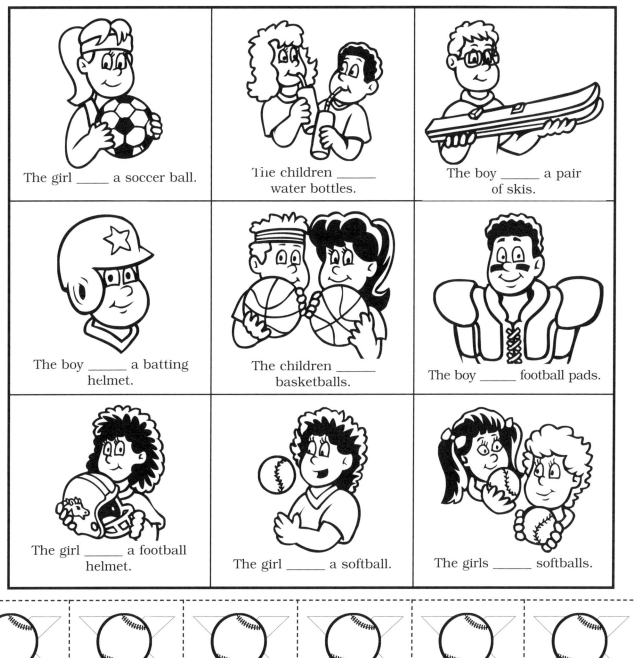

The girl _____ a soccer ball.	The children _____ water bottles.	The boy _____ a pair of skis.
The boy _____ a batting helmet.	The children _____ basketballs.	The boy _____ football pads.
The girl _____ a football helmet.	The girl _____ a softball.	The girls _____ softballs.

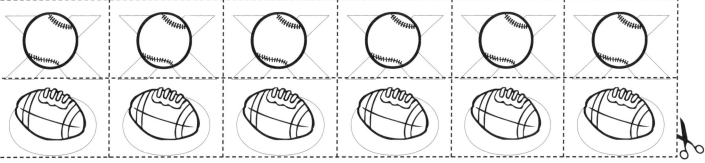

Homework Partner   Date

Game Board 9

Has/Have

Have/Has Locker

Directions: Cut the slot at the top of each locker. Then cut out the pictures on page 151. Place all cards face down on the table. Choose a card and complete the sentence, using "**have**" or "**has**" as appropriate. Then, fold and put each card through the slot of the correct locker. Continue until all cards have been read.

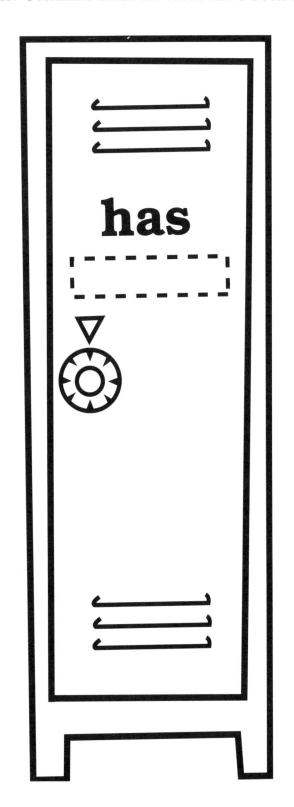
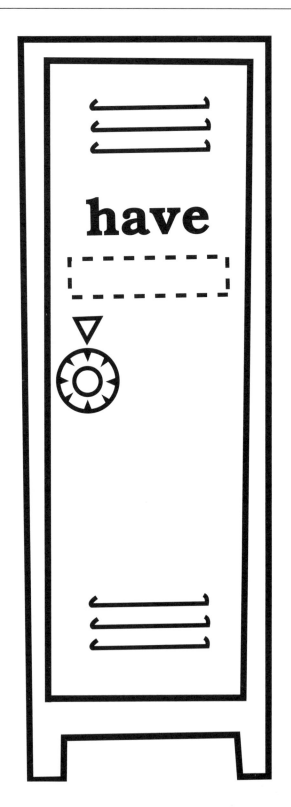

Homework Partner   Date

Game Board 9
Has/Have

150   #BK-298 Grammar Game Board Fun Sheets • ©2002 Super Duper® Publications • 1-800-277-8737 • Online! www.superduperinc.com

Have/Has Locker Cards

Directions: Cut out the cards below. Then, follow the instructions on page 150.

The boy _____ a hockey stick.

The boy _____ a basketball.

The children _____ bats.

The children _____ baseball caps.

The girl _____ a football helmet.

The girl _____ a football.

The boy _____ tennis shoes.

The boy _____ ice skates.

The children _____ hockey sticks.

The girl _____ a volleyball.

The children _____ mitts.

The girl _____ a soccer ball.

_____ _____
Homework Partner   Date

Game Board 9

Has/Have

Sports Talk Coloring

Directions: Listen to or read the sentences below. Complete each sentence with "**have**" or "**has**." Color the correct helmet. Then, read each sentence correctly.

1. The children (have / has) cleats.

2. The girl (have / has) a volleyball.

3. The boy (have / has) a tennis racquet.

4. The children (have / has) mitts.

5. The children (have / has) hockey pucks.

6. The boy (have / has) a fishing pole.

7. The children (have / has) hockey sticks.

8. The girl (have / has) a softball.

9. The girl (have / has) a football.

10. The boy (have / has) a golf club.

_____ _____
Homework Partner   Date

Game Board 9
Has/Have

Sports Day

Directions: Read or listen to the story below. Complete the sentences using "**have**" or "**has**."

It is "Sports Day" in Ms. Jones' class today. Each student is talking about his or her favorite sport. Each child _____ the equipment used to play that sport, too. Bobby is first. He _____ a fishing pole. "Fishermen _____ tackle boxes to hold extra hooks," Bobby says. Tom is second. "My football team is the best! The boys _____ helmets and football pads so they don't get hurt," he says. Next, it is Lucy's turn. She _____ a mitt. "Can you guess my sport? Right! My sport is softball!" she exclaims. "All the girls _____ water bottles, too," she adds. Finally, it is Christine's turn. She _____ a red uniform on a hanger. "Soccer players _____ cleats and soccer balls at every game," she says. Ms. Jones clapped loudly. "Great job, everyone," she says to the children, "I'm glad my children _____ so much fun playing sports!" She _____ a big smile for each child as they go out to play their favorite sports.

Homework Partner

Date

Game Board 9

Has/Have

Have/Has Olympics

Directions: Look at the scene below. Find and circle the following: children with water bottles; boy with tennis racquet; children with cleats; girl with soccer ball; boy with golf club; and girl with softball. Say each circled picture in a sentence. (The children **have** water bottles.)

Game Board 9
Has/Have

Homework Partner _____ Date _____

Move the Football Up the Field

Directions: Cut out the football below. Place the football at the bottom of the page. Read or listen to each sentence and complete it using "**have**" or "**has**." Move the football up to the next sentence. Continue until you have completed every sentence. _____

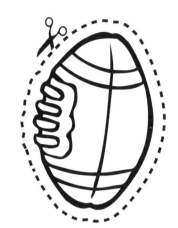

1. The children _____ tennis shoes.

2. The boy _____ a hockey stick.

3. The children _____ tennis shoes.

4. The girl _____ a softball.

5. The children _____ basketballs.

6. The children _____ water bottles.

7. The boy _____ a pair of skis.

8. The boy _____ a batting helmet.

9. The girl _____ a volleyball.

10. The children _____ cleats.

_____   _____   Game Board 9
Homework Partner   Date   **Has/Have**

Tennis Anyone?

Directions: Cut out the pictures at the bottom of the page. Glue/tape or place them onto and around the tennis player. Say a "**has**" sentence about each item. (She **has** a skirt.)

Homework Partner   Date   Has/Have

Sports Talk Listening

Directions: Listen to each sentence below. If the sentence is **correct**, color the safe. If the sentence is **incorrect**, color the out. Then, read the sentence correctly.

1. The goalie **has** goalie gloves.

2. The catcher **have** a catcher's mask.

3. The basketball players **has** a hoop.

4. Fishermen **have** tackle boxes.

5. A golfer **have** a golf bag.

6. An ice skater **has** a costume.

7. A tennis player **has** a bucket of tennis balls.

8. Football players **has** a jersey.

9. Volleyball players **have** a net.

10. The skier **have** ski boots.

_____ _____
Homework Partner   Date

Has/Have

Have/Has Bats

Directions: Read and complete the sentence in each bat using "**have**" or "**has**." Color the "**have**" bats green. Color the "**has**" bats yellow. Then, read each sentence correctly.

1. Skiers _____ ski poles.

2. A goalie _____ a goal net.

3. Football players _____ jerseys.

4. The roller blader _____ roller blades.

5. The golfers _____ golf tees.

6. A baseball player _____ a uniform.

7. A basketball player _____ a hoop.

8. A soccer player _____ shin guards.

Homework Partner   Date   Has/Have

Search

Directions: If you prefer, glue this page to construction paper for added durability. Cut out all the cards below. Shuffle and place them in a pile face down. Remove one card. This is the "search" card. Place face up. First player turns over the top card and completes the sentence using **has/have**. Take turns until someone turns over the card that matches the "search" card. That player wins! Pick another "search" card and play again until the pile is gone.

Homework Partner   Date   Has/Have

Fisherman's Maze

Directions: Help the fisherman catch the fish! Complete each sentence using **has/have** as you travel up stream.

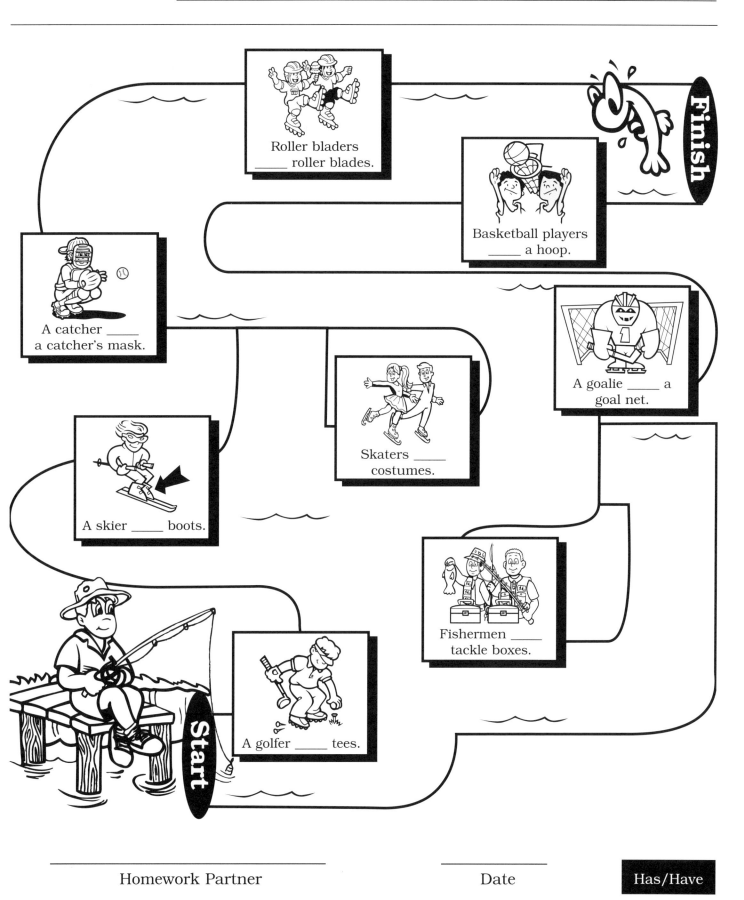

Homework Partner　　　　　Date　　　　　Has/Have

Double Spinner Fun

Directions: If you prefer, glue this page to construction paper for added durability. Cut out the arrows and dials below. Use a brad to connect the arrows to the dials. Spin both spinners. Spinner one tells you to use "**has**" or "**have**." Spinner two tells you another word to use in your sentence. (Basketball players **have** a hoop.) (A basketball player **has** a hoop.)

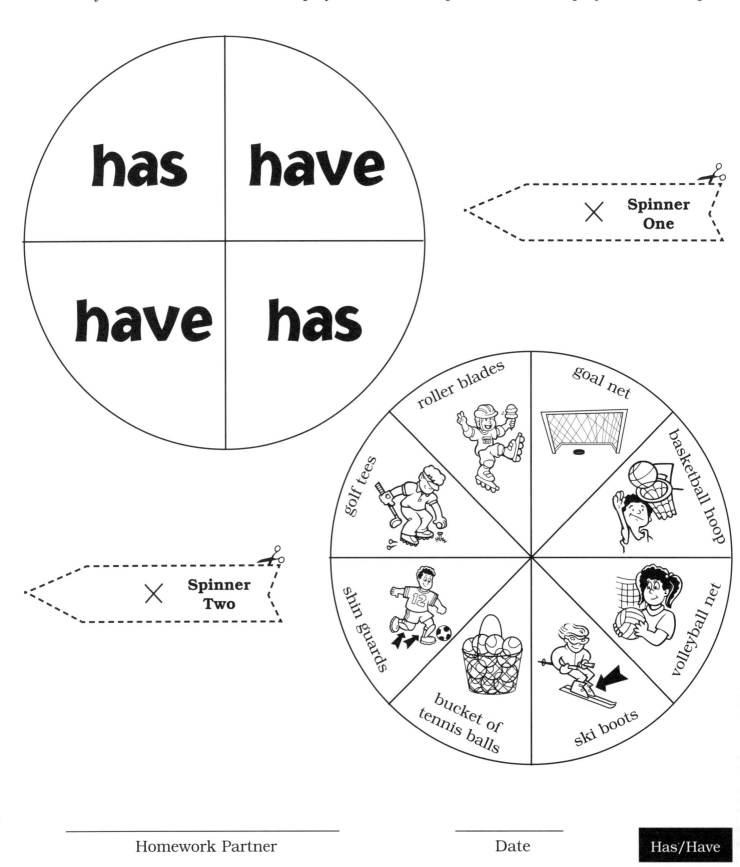

Whose Is It? Animal Match

Directions: Draw a line from each animal to two items that belong to that animal. Say a sentence for each item. (This is the dog's bone.)

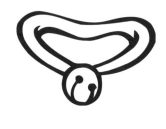

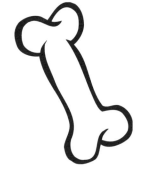

Homework Partner　　　Date

Game Board 10

Possessive Nouns

Pet Day Spinner

Directions: If you prefer, glue this page to construction paper for added durability. Cut out the arrow/dial. Use a brad to connect the dial to the circle. Spin the spinner and tell who owns the item.

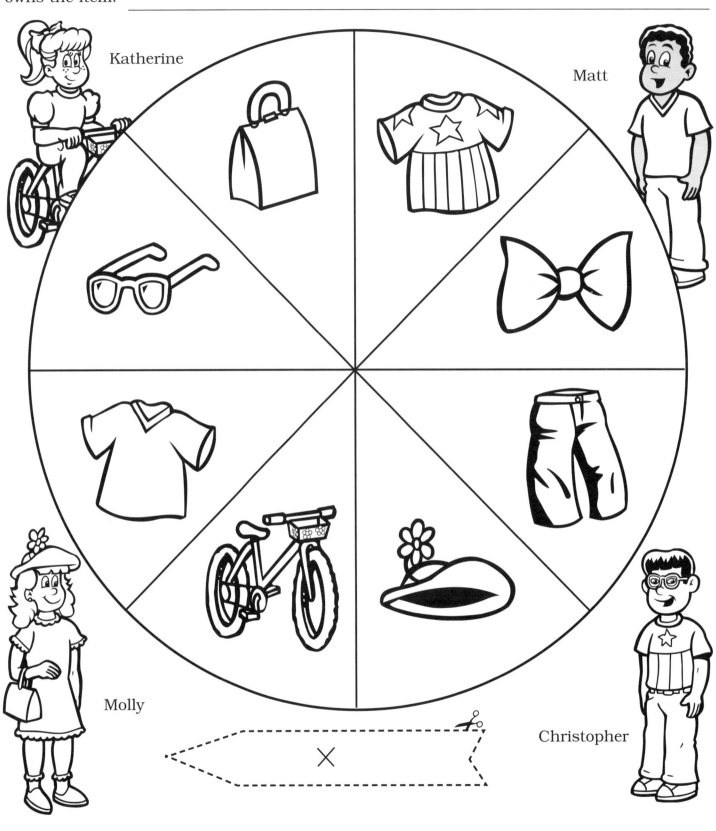

Homework Partner   Date

Game Board 10

Possessive Nouns

Pet Day Adventure

Directions: Read the story or have your helper read it to you. Look at the picture and say that word. Don't forget to add "'**s**."

It was Pet Day at Super Duper School. The children and their pets arrived at school for the big day. Things started to get a little crazy when [Christopher]'s dog, Fido, ate the [rabbit]'s carrot. [Matt]'s rabbit was afraid, so it hopped into [Tim]'s lap. Tim laughed but [Tim]'s cat was angry and jumped onto the [parrot]'s cage. The bird escaped from the cage and landed on [Molly]'s hat. Then, the bird stole [Christopher]'s glasses. The only animal that did not get into trouble was [Katherine]'s pig. So Penelope Pig won the Best Pet Blue Ribbon. What a Pet Day adventure!

Circle and Say

Directions: Circle the correct owner of each item on the right. Read/say the sentence, adding the possessive ending. (This is Tim's hat.) _____

1. This is     .

2. This is the     .

3. This is     .

4. This is     .

5. This is (the)     .

_____   _____
Homework Partner   Date

Game Board 10

Possessive Nouns

Pet Day Puzzle

Directions: Cut out the puzzle pieces on page 171. Shuffle and place face down. Pick a puzzle piece and find the person or animal on this page that owns each object. Say a sentence about each picture. (This is Molly's hat.) _____

_____ _____
Homework Partner   Date

Game Board 10
Possessive Nouns

Pet Day Puzzle

Directions: Cut out and shuffle the puzzle pieces below. Follow the directions on page 170.

Homework Partner   Date

Game Board 10

Possessive Nouns

Add One More

Directions: Cut out the pictures at the bottom of the page. Glue/tape or place each picture onto the box at the end of each sentence. Say each sentence.

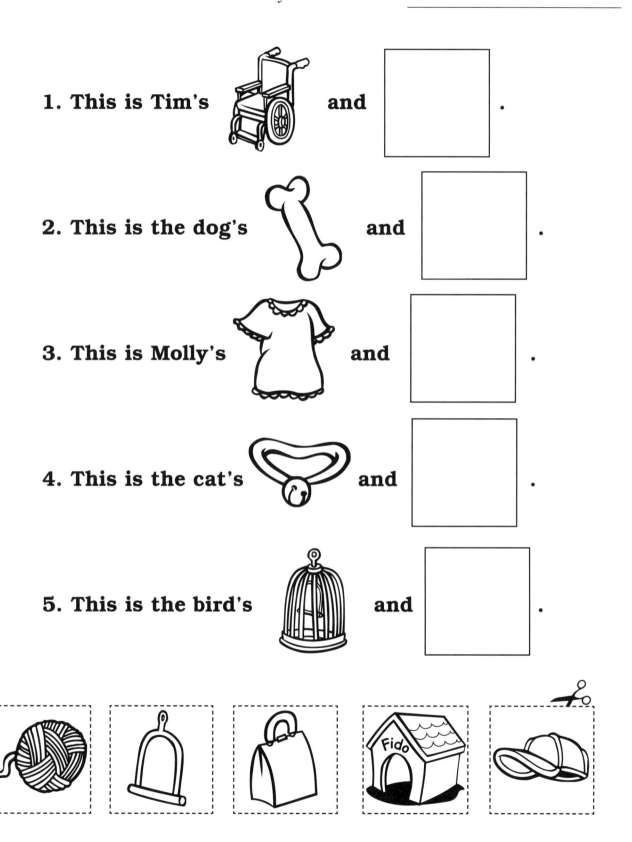

1. This is Tim's [wheelchair] and [ ].

2. This is the dog's [bone] and [ ].

3. This is Molly's [shirt] and [ ].

4. This is the cat's [collar] and [ ].

5. This is the bird's [cage] and [ ].

Homework Partner _____ Date _____

Game Board 10
Possessive Nouns

Pet Day Show and Tell

Directions: Cut out the circle and school house below. Cut out the window and door on the school house along the dotted lines. Attach the circle behind the school house with a brad. Spin the wheel and say the sentences aloud. Tell what you see in the window (Tim's...) and the door (...cat). (Don't forget the "**s**"!)

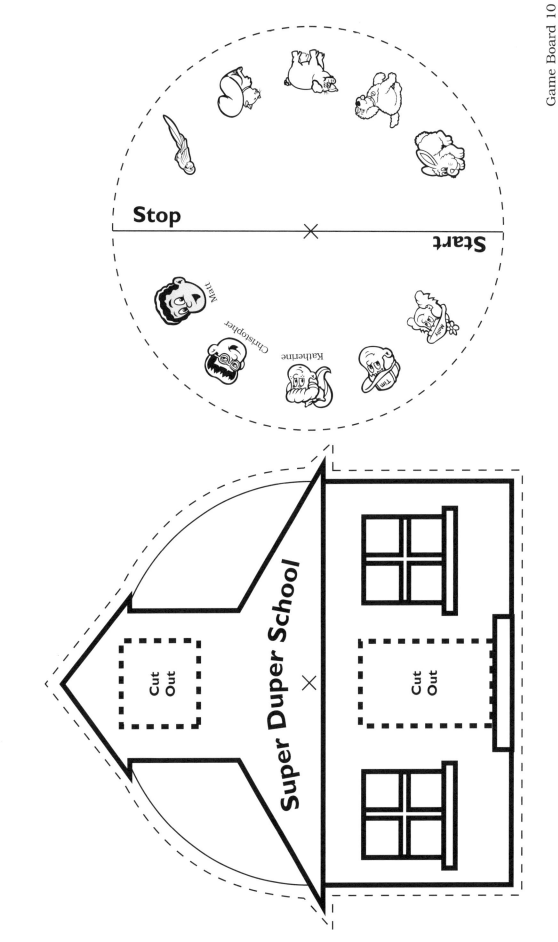

Game Board 10
Possessive Nouns

Homework Partner _____ Date _____

#BK-298 Grammar Game Board Fun Sheets • ©2002 Super Duper® Publications • 1-800-277-8737 • Online! www.superduperinc.com 173

Write the Possessive

Directions: Look at the picture on the left. Read the sentence. Complete the sentence with the correct possessive noun. (This is **Molly's** purse.)

1.  This is _____ purse.

2.  This is the _____ bone.

3.  This is _____ basket.

    Katherine

4.  This is the _____ collar.

5.  This is _____ wheelchair.

6.  This is the _____ swing.

7. This is _____ rabbit.

    Matt

Homework Partner   Date

Pet Day Match

Directions: Draw a line from the animal in Column A to the item that belongs to it in Column B. Say each sentence. (This is the turtle's _____.)

A   **B**

   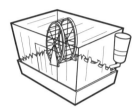

Homework Partner   Date   **Possessive Nouns**

Pet Day Lost and Found

Directions: Connect each person with his or her lost item. Say the possessive nouns in sentences. (It is **Ashley's** headband.) If you need a clue, look at the people at the bottom of the page.

Homework Partner   Date

Possessive Nouns

176   #BK-298 Grammar Game Board Fun Sheets • ©2002 Super Duper® Publications • 1-800-277-8737 • Online! www.superduperinc.com

Following Directions on Pet Day

Directions: Read or listen to the directions to color this page. When you have finished coloring, say a sentence about each person.

Danny's socks are green and his shorts are blue.
Greg's sweatshirt is brown and his skateboard is red.
Billy's backpack is blue and his scooter is orange.
Ashley's pants are yellow and her headband is blue.
Mary's shoes are brown and her dress is green.

Homework Partner _____ Date _____

Possessive Nouns

Pet Cube

Directions: Assemble the cube as follows. Glue onto construction paper for added durability. Cut on the dotted lines. Fold on solid lines and glue as indicated. To play: roll the cube. Look at the picture and word on the top side of the cube and name something that could belong to that animal. Then, make a sentence using the possessive form of the animal. (I opened the **hamster's** cage.) For a hint, use the pictures around the cube.

Homework Partner   Date

Possessive Nouns

Pet Day Game Board

Directions: Cut out the game markers below. Flip a coin to determine the number of spaces to move. Heads, move one space. Tails, move two spaces. As you land on each space, make up a sentence telling to whom or what the objects belong. Use the pictures on the left as clues. (This is the **turtle's** rock.)

Homework Partner _____ Date _____

Possessive Nouns

Drop a Penny

Directions: Drop a penny, name the item it lands on and say it in a sentence using the possessive form of the noun. (It is the **puppy's** bowl.)

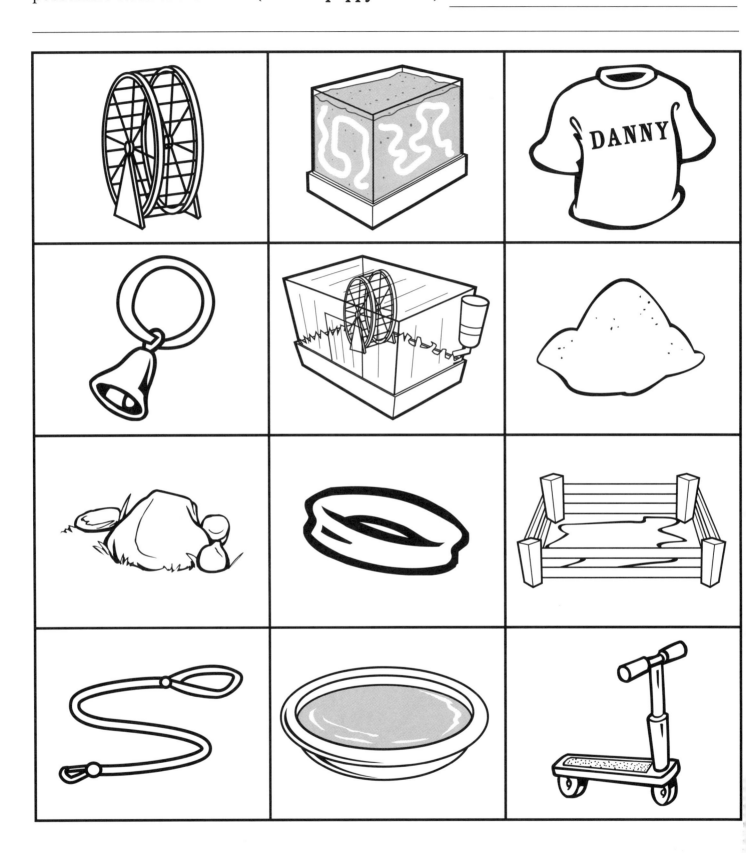

Homework Partner Date

Possessive Nouns

Form a Passive

Directions: Read the sentence. Fill in the blanks to correctly form the passive.

1. **The children sang a song.**
   _____ was sung by
   _____ .

2. **The bear found the honey.**
   _____ was found by
   _____ .

3. **The boy washed the dishes.**
   _____ were washed by
   _____ .

4. **The bird awakened the boy.**
   _____ was awakened by
   _____ .

5. **The boy zipped the sleeping bag.**
   _____ was zipped by
   _____ .

6. **The bee stung the girl.**
   _____ was stung by
   _____ .

Homework Partner   Date

Game Board 11

Passive Tense

Passive Fill-Ins

Directions: Read each sentence. Fill in the blank with the correct word to complete the passive sentence.

1. **The dog chased the mouse.**
   _____ was chased by the dog.

2. **The girl caught the fish.**
   _____ were caught by the girl.

3. **The boy patted the dog.**
   _____ was patted by the boy.

4. **The mouse nibbled the cheese.**
   _____ was nibbled by the mouse.

5. **The girl paddled the canoe.**
   _____ was paddled by the girl.

6. **The deer followed the rabbit.**
   _____ was followed by the deer.

_____   _____
Homework Partner   Date

Game Board 11

Passive Tense

More Passive Fill-Ins

Directions: Read each sentence. Complete each sentence using the passive form of the verb.

1. **The bear climbed the tree.**
   The tree _____.

2. **The boy chopped the wood.**
   The wood _____.

3. **The children pitched the tent.**
   The tent _____.

4. **The girl built the fire.**
   The fire _____.

5. **The boy piled the logs.**
   The logs _____.

6. **The children roasted the marshmallows.**
   The marshmallows _____
   _____.

_____   _____
        Homework Partner   Date

Match the Picture

Directions: Read/say each sentence. Then, draw a line to connect the passive sentence to the correct picture.

   The mouse **was chased** by the dog.

The dog **was chased** by the mouse.

   The fish **was caught** by the girl.

The girl **was caught** by the fish.

   The deer **was followed** by the rabbit.

The rabbit **was followed** by the deer.

   The boy **was watched** by the owl.

The owl **was watched** by the boy.

   The boy **was patted** by the dog.

The dog **was patted** by the boy.

Homework Partner   Date

Paste a Passive

Directions: Cut out the pictures at the bottom of the page. Read each sentence and find the picture that goes with it. Glue/tape or place the picture in the blank. Continue until all pictures are in place.

1. The can was opened by the girl.

2. The sandwich was eaten by the bear.

3. The boys were watched by the owl.

4. The fire was put out by the rain.

5. The lantern was lit by the boy.

Homework Partner   Date

Game Board 11

Passive Tense

Passive Sequencing

Directions: Cut out the pictures on the right side of the page. Keep the A's, B's, etc., together as sets. Pick a set of cards and put the sentence parts in the correct order. Glue/tape or place them in the boxes on the left side of the page. Read your sentence aloud. Repeat this activity with all five sentence strips.

A: The acorns | by the squirrel. | were gathered

B: was stung | by the bee. | The girl

C: by the boy. | The dog | was patted

D: was climbed | by the bear. | The tree

E: The logs | by the boy. | were piled

Homework Partner

Date

Game Board 11

Passive Tense

Passive Tic-Tac-Toe

Directions: Cut out the Tic-Tac-Toe tokens below. One player gets "**owls**" and the other gets "**raccoons**." Player one picks out a square, and makes a sentence about the picture using the passive form. (The dishes **were washed** by the boy.) Player one puts a token on the picture. Second player follows in turn. Three in a row wins.

washed	built	sung
chopped	counted	eaten
followed	zipped	chased

Homework Partner Date

Game Board 11

Passive Tense

Passive Spinner Activity

Directions: If you prefer, glue this page to construction paper for added durability. Cut out the arrow/dial. Use a brad to connect the dial to the circle. Spin the spinner. Say each sentence using the passive form. (The honey **was found** by the bear.)

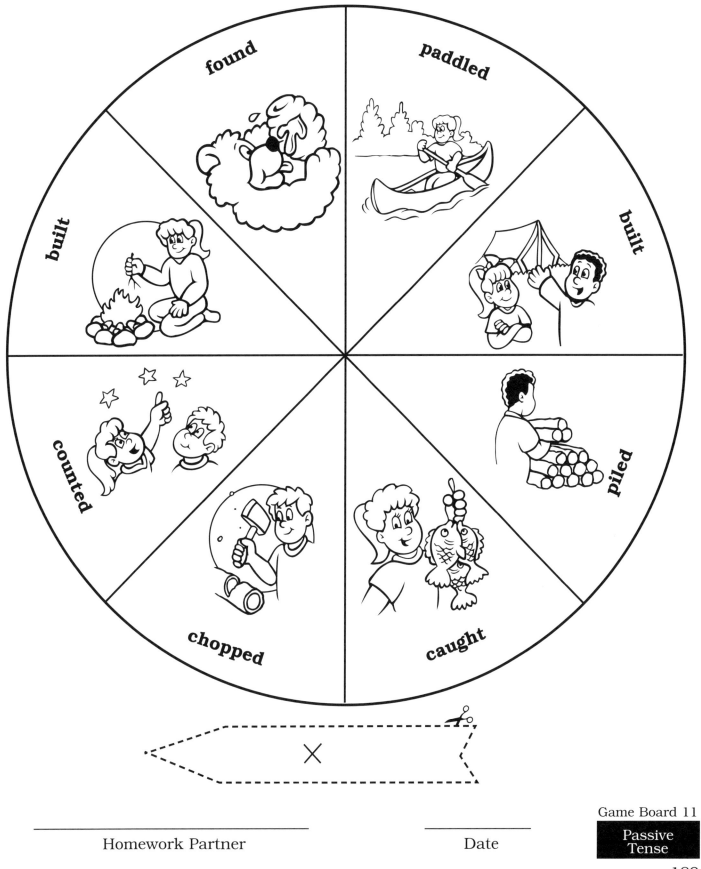

Homework Partner   Date

Game Board 11

Passive Tense

Passive Puzzle Fun

Directions: Cut out and shuffle the puzzle pieces on page 191 and place them face up. Pick a puzzle piece and say a sentence using the passive form. (The acorns **were gathered** by the squirrel.) Look for the passive verb on this page that matches the picture on your puzzle piece. Place the puzzle piece on the puzzle. Then, say the sentence.

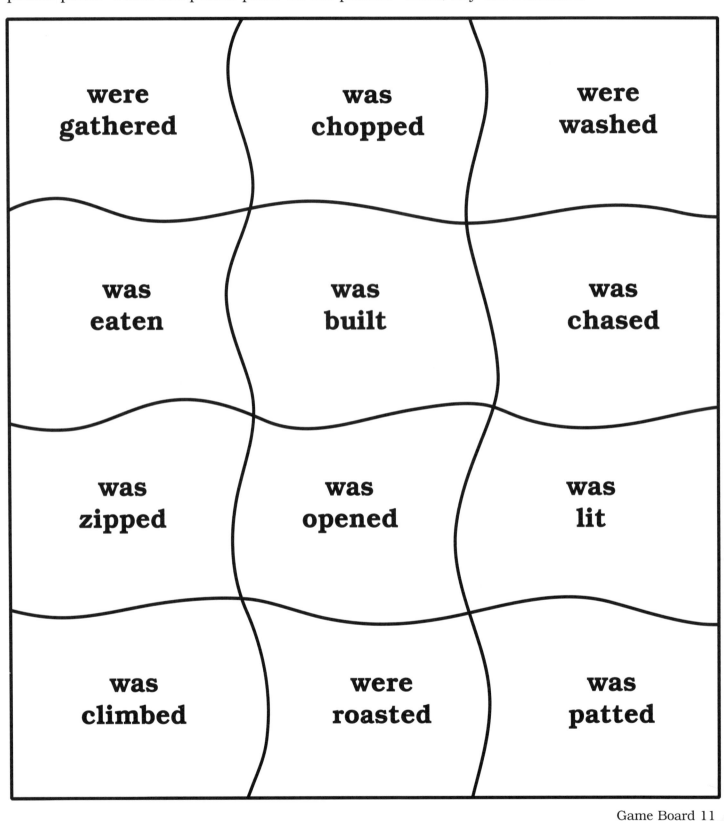

Game Board 11

Passive Tense

Puzzle Fun

Directions: Cut out and shuffle the puzzle pieces below. Then, follow the instructions on page 190.

Game Board 11

Passive Tense

Homework Partner   Date

Camp Scene

Directions: Find the following passive tense verbs in this scene: **was pitched by**, **were roasted by**, **was climbed by**, **was paddled by**, **was caught by**, **was chased by**. Use each phrase in a sentence. (The tent **was pitched by** the boy.) Circle each one.

Game Board 11
Passive Tense

Homework Partner _____ Date _____

Passive Memory

Directions: If you prefer, glue this page onto construction paper for added durability. Cut out all the cards. Place the picture cards face down in one group and the word cards in another group. Take turns flipping one card from each group trying to match the pictures to the passive phrase. Whoever has the most matches at the end of the game wins.

	were piled by		was climbed by
	were roasted by		was seen by
	was made by		was heard by
	was stolen by		were hung by

Homework Partner　　　　Date

Passive Tense

Color a Star Passive Activity

Directions: Read/say each sentence aloud. Change each sentence to the passive form. Then, color a star and read/say the sentence using the passive form. (The scary stories **were told** by the children.)

1. The children told scary stories.

2. The girl collected the sticks.

3. The boy wore the fishing hat.

4. Joe tied the canoe.

5. Mary saw the bat.

6. The girl hung the bathing suits on the tree branch.

7. The dog heard the owl.

8. The raccoon stole the hot dog.

9. The girl climbed the mountain.

Homework Partner   Date

Passive Tense

Choose a Picture

Directions: Cut out the pictures at the bottom of the page along the dotted line. Read each sentence and choose the picture that is being described in the sentence. Glue/tape or place the picture in the box at the end of each sentence. _____

1. The mouse was chased by the dog.

2. The dog was petted by the boy.

3. The boy was seen by the owl.

4. The deer was followed by the rabbit.

Homework Partner   Date

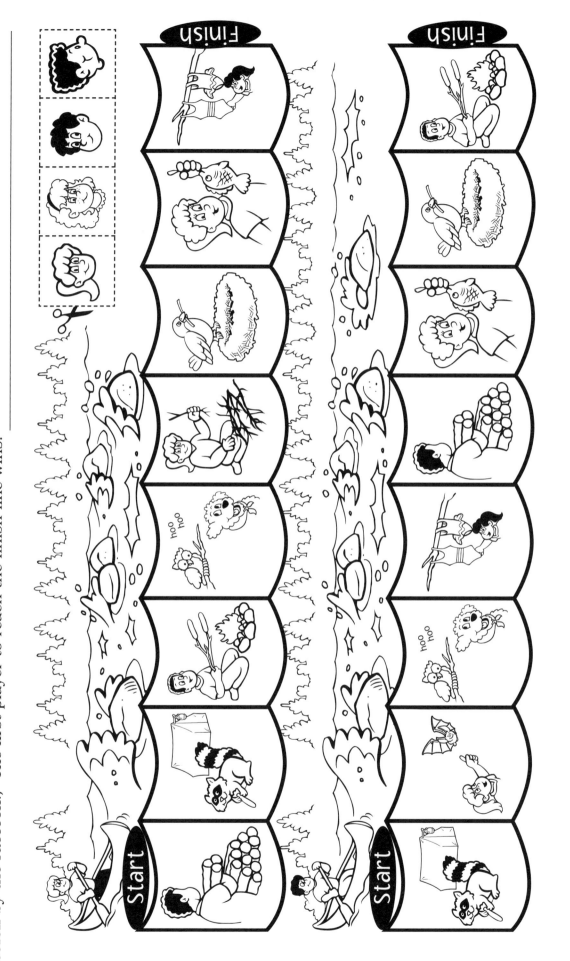

Fire and Ice

Directions: Have your partner pick a picture on this page, but tell him/her not to tell you what it is. Then, try to figure out which picture your partner chose by asking questions using the passive form. (The tree **was climbed** by the bear?) If the picture you chose is close to target, your partner should say, "You are hot." If it is far away from the target, he/she should say, "You are cold." Keep trying until you guess your partner's picture. Then, switch places.

Homework Partner   Date

Passive Tense

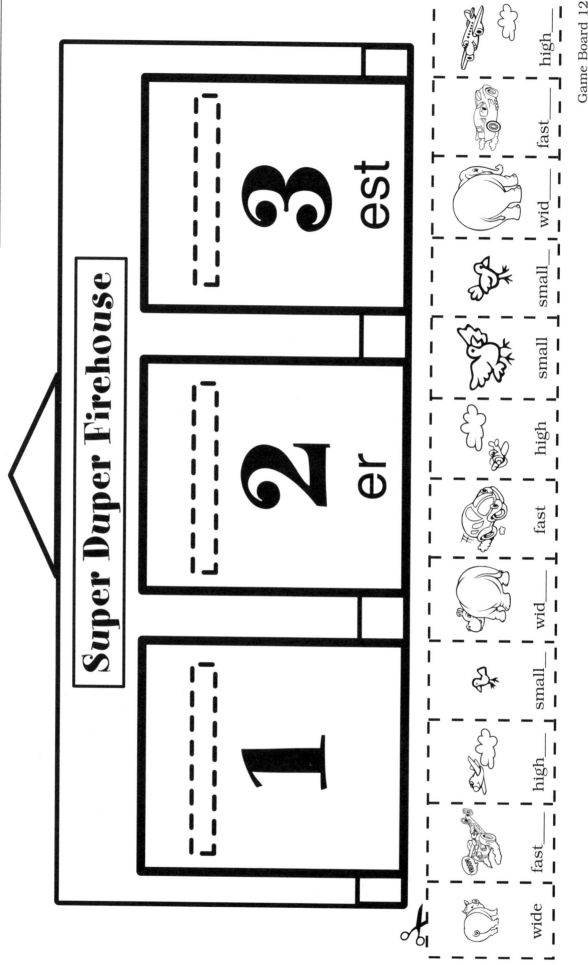

Comparative/Superlative Tic-Tac-Toe

Instructions: Cut out the Tic-Tac-Toe tokens below. One player gets "**hydrants**" and the other gets "**stop signs**." Take turns covering a picture and saying the comparative (**er**) and superlative (**est**) form of each base word (**heavy, heavier, heaviest**). Three in a row wins!

heavy	wet	high
slow	tall	small
young	short	loud

Homework Partner   Date

Game Board 12
Comparatives & Superlatives

Paste An Ending

Directions: Cut out the "er" and "est" endings at the bottom of the page. Glue/tape or place the correct ending in the box below each picture. Then, say each word in a sentence.

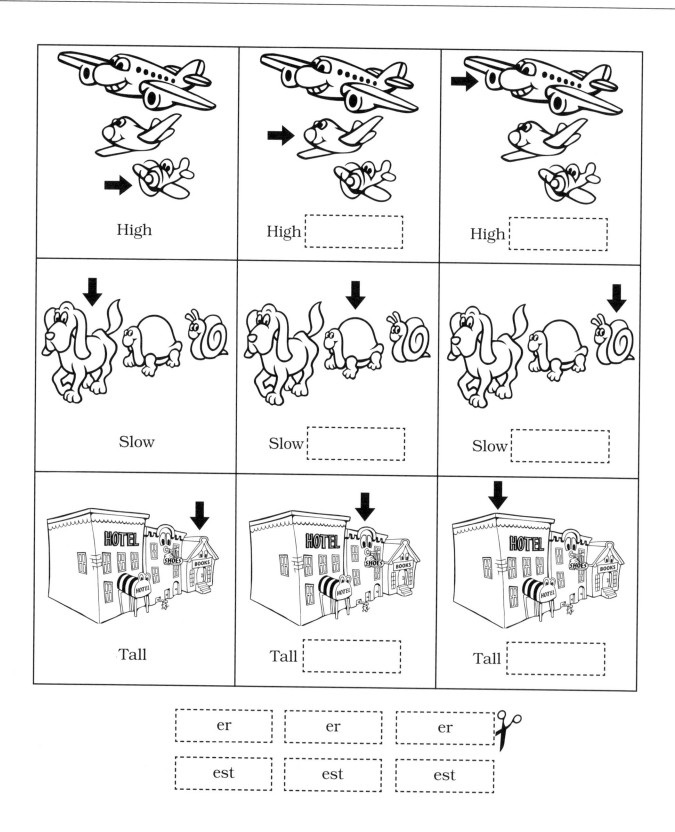

Game Board 12

Comparatives & Superlatives

Comparative/Superlative Spinner Activity

Directions: If you prefer, glue this page to construction paper for added durability. Cut out the arrow/dial. Use a brad to connect the dial to the circle. Spin the spinner. Say a sentence for the word indicated on the spinner, using the correct ending (er/est). (**The baby is the youngest child**.)

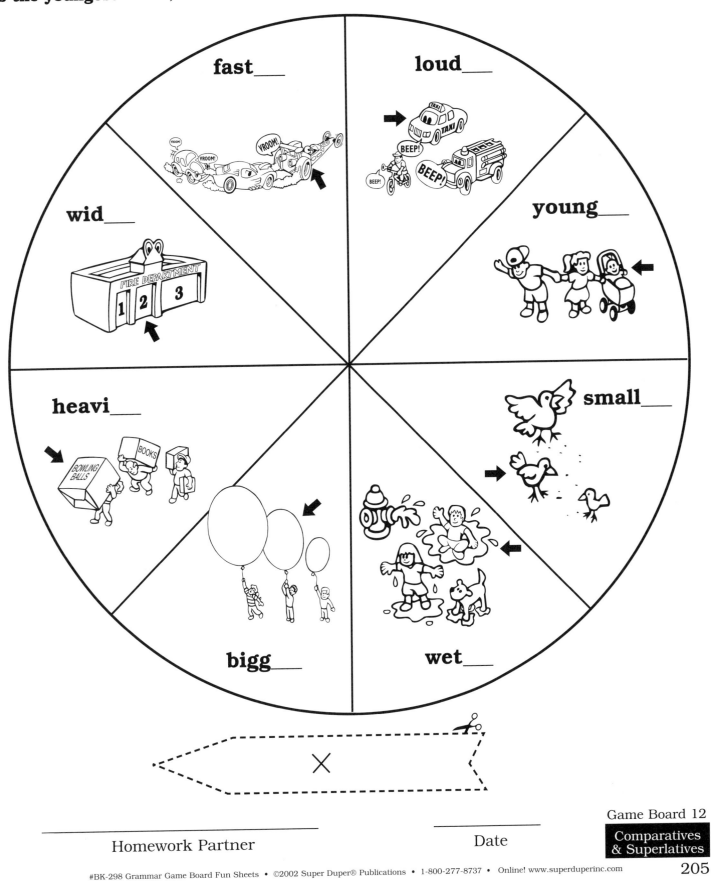

Homework Partner _____ Date _____

Game Board 12
Comparatives & Superlatives

Color Comparative Fun

Directions: Color the picture that matches the word on the left. Then, say a sentence for each "er" picture-word. (**The turtle is slower than the dog**.)

Color the one that is:

higher		
slower		
younger		
louder		
taller		
smaller		

Homework Partner   Date

Game Board 12

Comparatives & Superlatives

Circle a Word

Directions: Read each sentence. Circle the word that correctly completes each one. Write the word in the blank. Then, read each sentence aloud again. _____

1. An elephant is _____ than a mouse.
   (big, bigger, biggest)

2. A fire siren is the _____ sound of all.
   (loud, louder, loudest)

3. A golf ball is _____ than a basketball.
   (small, smaller, smallest)

4. A bowling ball is the _____ ball.
   (heavy, heavier, heaviest)

5. A boy is _____, but an infant is even _____.
   (young, younger, youngest)   (young, younger, youngest)

6. My kite is _____ than your kite.
   (high, higher, highest)

7. A race car is the _____ car of all.
   (fast, faster, fastest)

8. Of Mary, Mike, and Sue, Sue is the _____.
   (tall, taller, tallest)

_____   _____
Homework Partner   Date

Game Board 12
Comparatives & Superlatives

City Scene - Following Directions

Directions: Color the <u>highest</u> bird blue. Color the <u>shorter</u> boy. Underline the <u>faster</u> car and circle the <u>fastest</u> car. Draw two windows on the <u>widest</u> building. Color the <u>tall</u> tree and draw a bird in the <u>taller</u> tree. Circle the <u>tallest</u> tree. Color the <u>bigger</u> balloon red and the <u>biggest</u> balloon yellow.

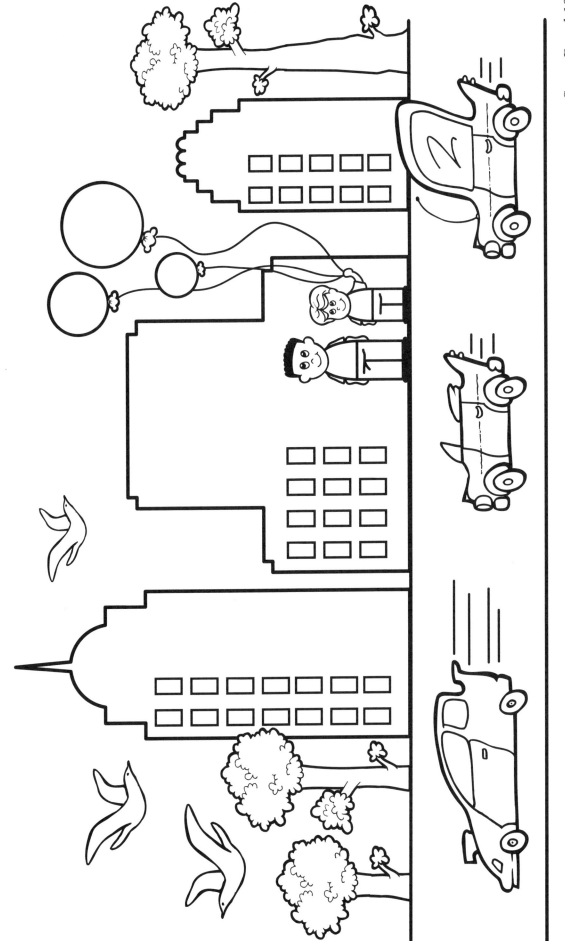

Homework Partner _____   Date _____

Game Board 12

Comparatives & Superlatives

Fold a Dog

Directions: Color the dog and cut it out along the dotted line. Next fold along the lines so that the ● touches the ● and the ✗ touches the ✗. Start out with the "long" dog. Say, "This dog is long." Now, pull the tail to unfold one flap. Say, "This dog is longer." Finally, pull the tail all the way. Say, "This dog is longest."

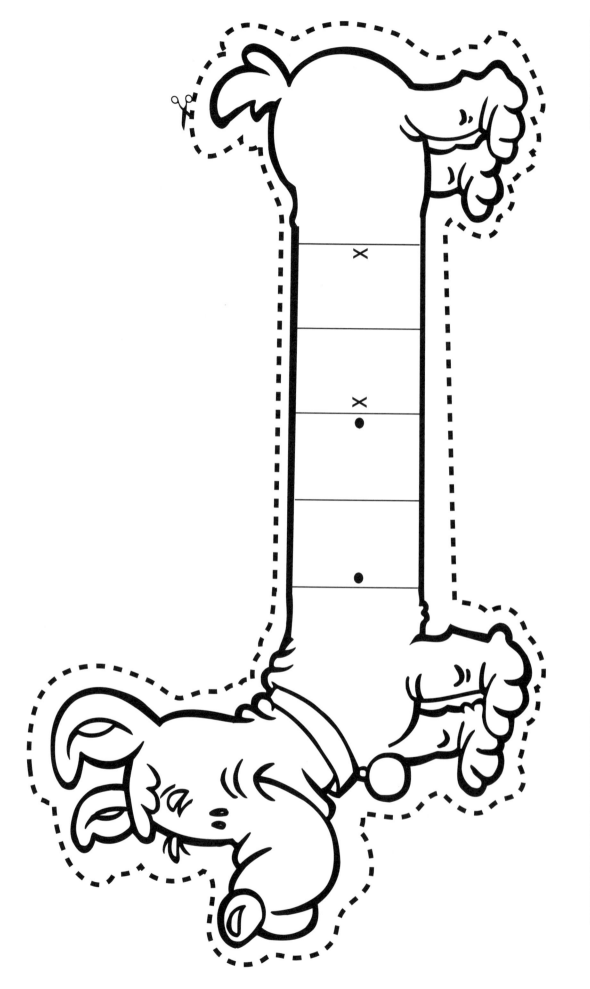

Comparatives & Superlatives

Homework Partner

Date

Puzzle Fun

Directions: Cut out and shuffle the puzzle pieces on page 213 and place face up. Pick a puzzle piece and say the word. Then say the comparative (**er**) form of that word (**few–fewer**). Find the picture on this page that shows the comparative (**er**) form. Then, place the puzzle piece on the puzzle.

Homework Partner   Date

Comparatives & Superlatives

Color a Superlative

Directions: Color the picture in each row that is the:

fewest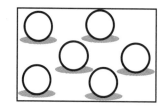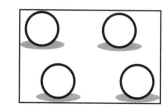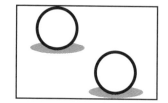

lightest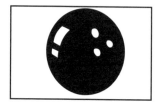

darkest

dirtiest

longest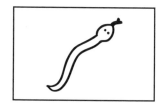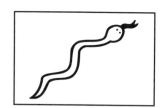

narrowest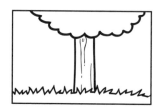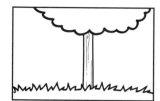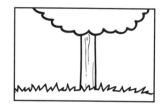

Homework Partner   Date

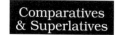

Listening For Comparatives & Superlatives

Directions: Read or listen to each sentence. If the sentence is **correct**, color the **green light**. If the sentence is **incorrect**, color the **red light** and say the sentence correctly.

1. Main street is the **bumpiest** road in town.

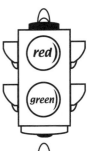

2. My hair is **longer** than yours.

3. Yesterday, it was **cloudiest** than today.

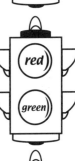

4. A feather is **lighter** than a cup.

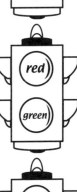

5. Summer is **hottest** than winter.

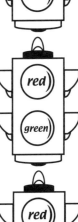

6. You are the **dirtier** of all the boys.

Homework Partner   Date

Answer Key

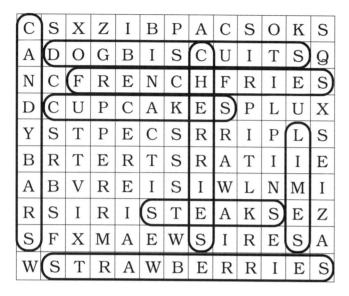

page 12

page 28

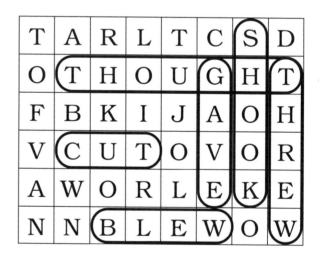

page 70

page 138